http://www.inputoutput.de

Editors:
Florian Pfeffer Germany I **Dieter Kretschmann** Germany

Contributing Editors:
Sheila de Bretteville USA I **Irma Boom** Netherlands I **Richard Doust** Great-Britain I **Neil Grant** Great-Britain I **Steven Heller** USA I **Ken Hiebert** USA I **Werner Jeker** Switzerland I **Eckhard Jung** Germany I **William Longhauser** USA I **Hanny Kardinata** Indonesia I **John Kortbawi** Lebanon I **Leila Musfy** Lebanon I **Peter Rea** Great-Britain I **Louise Sandhaus** USA I **Ahn Sang-Soo** Korea I **Robyn Stacey** Australia I **Chris Treweek** Great-Britain I **Teal Triggs** Great-Britain

:output presents works by students from all over the world.

Stu|dium *(lat.: studies)*
1. Striving, eagerness, sympathy, lust, desire
2. Devotion, sympathy, interest
3. Favorite pass-time, passion

2 | 3

Things you should know about this book...

**Florian Pfeffer +
Dieter Kretschmann**

:output zeigt Arbeiten von Studentinnen und Studenten aus aller Welt.

Stu|dium *(lat.: studies)*
  1. Bestreben, Eifer, Zuneigung, Lust, Begierde
  2. Ergebenheit, Zuneigung, Interesse
  3. Lieblingsbeschäftigung, Passion

Vi|sion
1. Seeing
2. optical hallucination
3. image designed with respect to something in the future

There are 236 countries in the world.

If there are an average of 10 graphic design colleges in each country and if approximately 100 students registered at every college and if every student makes about 4 designs per year, this results in 920.000 designs per year that are hardly ever seen by anyone.

We want to change that:
We make the invisible visible and present tomorrow's designers to you today.

Things you should know about this book...

Florian Pfeffer +
Dieter Kretschmann

Es gibt 236 Länder auf der Erde.

Wenn es in jedem Land durchschnittlich 10 Hochschulen für Grafik-Design gibt und an jeder Hochschule durchschnittlich 100 Studenten eingeschrieben sind und jeder Student im Jahr durchschnittlich 4 Entwürfe anfertigt, ergibt dies eine Anzahl von 920.000 pro Jahr, die allerdings kaum jemand zu Gesicht bekommt.

Das wollen wir ändern:
Wir machen Unsichtbares sichtbar und stellen Ihnen heute die Designer von morgen vor.

Vi|sion
1. Das Sehen
2. optische Halluzination
3. in Bezug auf Zukünftiges entworfenes Bild

Dif|ference
1. dissimilarity, variety
2. disagreement, discrepancy

In this book we present 107 projects by students from 18 countries with their own cultural backgrounds and different visual languages.

6 | 7
Things you should know about this book…
Florian Pfeffer + Dieter Kretschmann

Unter|schied, Dif|ferenz
1. Verschiedenheit
2. Meinungsverschiedenheit, Unstimmigkeit

Wir stellen Ihnen in diesem Buch 107 Projekte von Studenten aus 18 Ländern mit ihren jeweils eigenen kulturellen Hintergründen und unterschiedlichen visuellen Sprachen vor.

Ex|peri|ment *(lat.)*
  1. test, presentation, experience
  2. daring undertaking

8 | 9

Things you should know about this book...

Florian Pfeffer +
Dieter Kretschmann

Ex|peri|ment(*lat.*)
1. Versuch, Vorführung, Erfahrung
2. gewagtes Unternehmen

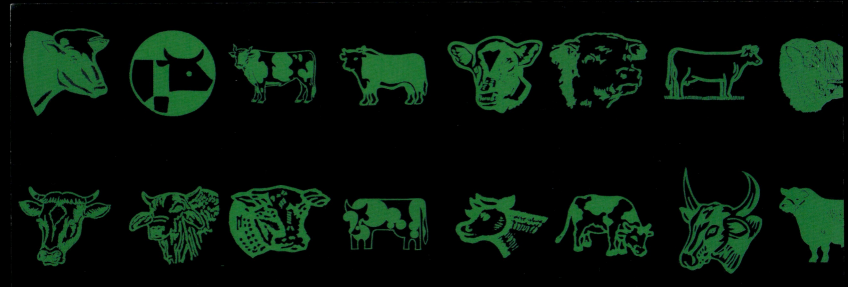

choice
1. decision, possiblity, alternative
2. vote

Submissions by students
It is important to us that all students can submit their own designs without pre-selection.

We want to thank our jury members who have made the selection from the 2.500 submitted slides.

The submissions selected by the jury are marked in the book with a magnifying glass.

Submissions by editors
Additionally, we offer colleges the possibility to present themselves and their students' works.

For this reason, we have invited professors from international colleges to become active as editors for :output and to make their own selection from the submissions by the students.

The submissions selected by the editors are marked in the book with an index finger.

**Contributing Editors:
Redakteure:**

Sheila de Bretteville
Irma Boom
Richard Doust
Neil Grant
Steven Heller
Ken Hiebert
Werner Jeker
Eckhard Jung
William Longhauser
Hanny Kardinata
John Kortbawi
Leila Musfy
Peter Rea
Louise Sandhaus
Ahn Sang-Soo
Robyn Stacey
Chris Treweek
Teal Triggs

Things you should know about this book...

Florian Pfeffer + Dieter Kretschmann

Einsendungen von Studenten
Es ist uns wichtig, daß alle Studenten ihre eigenen Entwürfe ohne Vorauswahl einsenden können.

Wir möchten uns bei unseren Jury-Mitgliedern bedanken, die die Auswahl aus den 2.500 eingesandten Dias getroffen haben.

Die Beiträge, die von der Jury ausgewählt wurden, sind mit einer Lupe gekennzeichnet.

Einsendungen von Redakteuren
Weiterhin geben wir auch den Hochschulen die Möglichkeit, sich und die Arbeiten ihrer Studenten darzustellen.

Aus diesem Grund haben wir Professorinnen und Professoren aus internationalen Hochschulen eingeladen, als Redakteure für :output tätig zu werden und zusätzlich zu den Einsendungen der Studenten eine eigene Auswahl zu treffen.

Die Beiträge, die von den Redakteuren ausgewählt wurden, sind mit einem Zeigefinger gekennzeichnet.

Jury:

Irma Boom, Amsterdam
Sheila de Bretteville, Yale University, School of Arts, New Haven
Werner Jeker, Lausanne
Florian Pfeffer, Bremen
Peter Rea, London, Beirut, Bremen
Erik Spiekermann, Berlin
Teal Triggs, London College of Printing

Wahl
1. Entscheidung, Möglichkeit, Alternative
2. Abstimmung

Damir Gamulin

Rusko Mesko: Russian Meat: Visual identity for a movie
Erscheinungsbild für einen Film

Professor:
Nenad Dogan

College:
**School of Design
Faculty of Architecture and Design
University of Zagreb**

Study Year: **4**

selected by the jury

1 Poster (opposite page)
2 T-Shirt
3 Folder (example page)
4 Folder (example page)

Damir Gamulin:

The movie deals with brothels and organised crime during the war in Croatia. Almost everything in the movie seems glamorous with only a few bursts of violence until suddenly it ends in a mass killing and destruction.

What I wanted to achieve was not only to illustrate the story but also to get the ambience of the movie through the beautiful and warm red being corroded and eaten up.

End

Der Film handelt von dem organisiertem Verbrechen während des Krieges in Kroatien. Fast alle Bilder in dem Film strahlen eine glamouröse Stimmung aus. Es gibt nur einige wenige gewalttätige Szenen bis plötzlich alles in einem Massaker und Zerstörung endet.

Ich wollte in meiner Arbeit nicht nur die Geschichte illustrieren, sondern die Ambivalenz des Films durch ein schönes, warmes Rot zeigen, das angegriffen und aufgefressen wird.

Ende

film Lukáša Nolete

Ruská mesa

Sibylle Reichelt + Maike Truschkowski

Kassel: Imaginations
Kassel: Vorstellungen

Professor:
Christof Gassner
Jörg Stürzebecher

College:
Universität
Gesamthochschule
Kassel

Study Year: **5/6**

selected by the jury

Prof. Christof Gassner:

Something that's right at the center of things can't be totally out of it, since there are not only »15 underpasses« in Kassel but also »15 swans in the park« and which town can keep up with that aside from »13 cinemas« also »2 (cartoon movie) Oscars«. There's also »Ahle Worscht, Kimmerkarduffeln« and the insight: »The natural enemy of the North Hessians is the South Hessian.«

The theme of Sibylle Reichelt and Maike Truschkowski's graduate work is communication in public spaces, the auditory and visual perception of everyday life – language, sounds, images and symbols in public space. This is explained in the example of Kassel: here, the two designers studied visual communication.

In dozens of interviews, the people of Kassel (Kasseler, Kasselaner and Kasseläner – the three levels of Kassel identity) were asked about their town. They asked the mayor and numerous craftsmen, urban planners and house cleaners, regional poets and crack ice hockey players. They collected hundreds of statements, in the streets and squares, the markets and passages, on the University campus and in bureaucratic offices. Here, they documented sounds and images of everyday life along a tram line that crosses the town.

»At first sight you see an image determined by gaps. Only at second glance does it condense and become accessible as an urban structure, an arrangement with a specific order...«
»Auf den ersten Blick sieht man ein von Lücken bestimmtes Bild. Erst auf den zweiten Blick verdichtet es sich und erschließt sich als Stadtstruktur, als Gefüge mit einer bestimmten Ordnung...«

»...Well, at first they can't say a word, it's a dialect that essentially consists of saying nothing....«
»...Also erst mal kriegen sie kein Wort raus. Es ist eine Mundart, die im Wesentlichen darin besteht, daß man nichts sagt...«

Sibylle Reichelt and Maike Truschkowski lead the quintessential nature of their widely positioned work back into the town, into public space, into every-day life. On the tram, they confront passengers with the Kassel-esque ideas of fellow citizens through a typographic installation; they confront radio listeners with Kassel sound collages on the public radio station. And pub visitors can follow the course and sounds on postcard images.

»Kassel: Vorstellungen«: Interactive verbal and visual communication in urban spaces. Insights and vistas of and about Kassel. Among the insights: »It takes the second glance«.

Was mitten drin liegt, kann nicht voll daneben sein, gibt es doch in Kassel nicht nur »15 Unterführungen«, sondern auch »15 Schwäne im Auepark« und – welche Stadt kann da mithalten – neben »13 Kinos« auch »2 (Trickfilm-) Oscars«. Weiter gibt es »Ahle Worscht, Kimmerkarduffeln« und die Erkenntnis: »Der natürliche Feind des Nordhessen ist der Südhesse«

Thema der Abschlußarbeit von Sibylle Reichelt und Maike Truschkowski ist die Kommunikation im öffentlichen Raum, ist die auditive und visuelle Wahrnehmung des Alltags, sind Sprache, Geräusche und Klänge, sind Bilder und Zeichen im öffentlichen Raum. Explizit wird das am Beispiel von Kassel: Hier studierten die beiden Gestalterinnen visuelle Kommunikation, hier fragten sie, in dutzenden von Interviews, Kasseler, Kasselaner und Kasseläner (das sind die drei Stufen Kasseler Identität) nach ihrer Stadt, befragten Oberbürgermeister und Handwerker, Stadtplaner und -reiniger, Heimatdichter und Eishockeycracks; hier sammelten sie auf Straßen und Plätzen, auf Märkten und Passagen, auf dem Campus und in Amtsstuben hunderte von Statements. Hier dokumentierten sie – entlang einer Straßenbahnlinie, die quer durch die Stadt führt – Geräusche und Bilder des Alltags.

Die Quintessenz ihrer breit angelegten Arbeit führen Sibylle Reichelt und Maike Truschkowski wieder in die Stadt, in den öffentlichen Raum, in den Alltag zurück: den Fahrgast konfrontieren sie mit den Kasseler Vorstellungen seiner Mitbürger durch eine typografische Installation in der Straßenbahn, den Radiohörer durch Kassel-O-Ton Collagen im offenen Kanal. Und der Keipenbesucher kann die Fahrt und die Geräusche auf Postkarten-Bildern nachvollziehen.

»Kassel: Vorstellungen«: Interaktive verbale und visuelle Kommunikation im Stadtraum. Ein- und Ansichten über Kassel. Unter den Einsichten auch diese: »Man braucht den zweiten Blick«.

»It would suit this town well to express a bit of intimacy, eroticism and sentiment...«
»Es würde dieser Stadt gut stehen, ein bißchen Initmität, Erotik und Gefühl zu zeigen...«

„Ich kann es nachmachen. Wenn ich dann den Unterkiefer vorschiebe und irgendsowas sage wie: „Is d`r Ridde däh?", dann sagt meine Frau sofort: „Hör bloß auf, das ist ja furchtbar!"

Desire and Pain
Lust und Leid

Jan Haux

Professor:
Gunter Rambow

College:
Hochschule für Gestaltung Karlsruhe

Study Year: **3**

selected by the jury

Country

Desire and Pain is a postcard project that evolved from the seminar »Topography of the Body«.

Lust und Leid ist ein Postkartenprojekt, das im Rahmen des Seminars »Topografie des Körpers« entstanden ist.

Polly Bertram:

The term »sampling« is haunting linguistic usage without a goal. The opinions about what sampling is and what its methodology and appearance are differ considerably.

The work has the goal to assist the clarification through the exemplification with auditory and visual means on basic hypotheses and offer us definitions of the term. In an entertaining way the boundary of the term itself is marked off, analogies and differences between audible and visual sampling become clear, and, simultaneously, the work offers an outlook on the possibilities of sampling.

Der Begriff »Sampling« geistert ziellos im Sprachgebrauch umher. Die Meinungen, was Sampling sei, was seine Methodik und seine Erscheinung, unterscheiden sich ganz beträchtlich. Die Arbeit setzt sich zum Ziel, zur Klärung beizutragen über die Exemplifizierung mit audiellen und visuellen Mitteln dreier grundlegender Thesen und Definitionen zum Begriff. Es wird auf unterhaltsame Weise die Grenze des Begriffs selber beschildert, Analogien und Unterschiede von audiellen und visuellem Sampling werden deutlich, und gleichzeitig bietet die Arbeit einen Ausblick auf die Möglichkeiten des Sampling.

Andreas Hidber >
Sampling

Professor:
Polly Bertram

College:
Schule für Gestaltung Zürich

selected by the jury

complete work on the CD-ROM

Country >

Divorce and Illiteracy
Scheidung und Analphabetismus

Kelly Stevens

Professor:
Henk van Assen

College:
The University of Texas at Austin

Study Year: 3

selected by the jury

Kelly Stevens:

Ein Mangel an Informationen über die Entwicklung der Lesefähigkeit von Kindern alleinerziehender Eltern brachte mich dazu, mich auf die Auswirkungen von Ehescheidungen auf die Lesefähigkeit von Kindern zu konzentrieren.

Entlang des Plakats verläuft eine Perforation an der Diagrammlinie, die die Familie »teilt«, wobei das Kind im Zentrum steht. Das Plakat soll ein Mailing sein, das an Familienberatungsstellen und Elternzentren verschickt wird. Auf der Rückseite des Plakats steht die Anweisung an den Empfänger, »das Plakat für Ausstellungszwecke durchzutrennen«.

Der Text lautet:
»Kinder aus geschiedenen Ehen im Vergleich zu Kindern aus intakten Familien
- werden eher in Sonderleseklassen verwiesen
- wiederholen eher eine Klasse
- haben einen niedrigeren IQ
- sind schlechter im Buchstabieren.
Kinder aus geschiedenen Ehen bedürfen der besonderen Fürsorge, um sicherzustellen, daß eine Scheidung die Zukunft des Kindes nicht kompromittiert. Kinder aus intakten Familien sind in 88,8% der Lesetests besser als Kinder alleinerziehender Eltern«.

Kelly Stevens:

A lack of available information regarding the reading development of children from one-parent homes led me to focus an the effects of divorce on children's reading skills.

Running the length of the poster is a perforation along the graph line that »splits« the family, with the child in the center.

The poster is intented to be a mailer send to family counseling and parenting centers. The mailing side of the poster instructs the recipient to »tear the poster in half for display«.

The text reads:
»Children of divorced families as compared to children of intact families:
- Are more likely to be referred to special reading classes
- More likely to repeat a class
- Have a lower IQ
- Lower spelling scores
Special care needs to be taken with children of divorced families to insure that divorce does not compromise the child's future. Children of two-parents homes surpass children from single-parent homes on 88,8% of reading test.«

Country

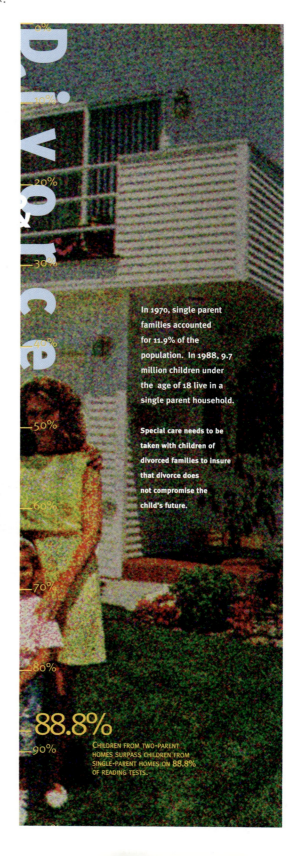

Katharina von Hellberg

Conversation with a stranger
Unterhaltung mit einem Fremden

Professor:
Patricia Sumner
Ian Noble

College:
London College of Printing

Study Year: **1**

selected by the jury

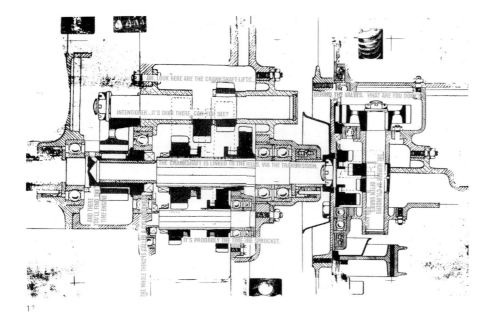

1

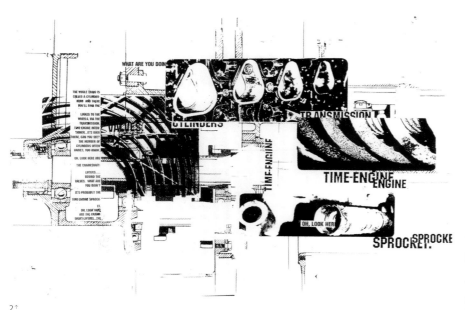

2

3

Katharina von Hellberg:

The poster series describes a conversation I had with a mechanic.

The first poster shows the technical explanation given by the mechanic.

On the second poster, we see how I try to decipher his explanation and mix it with my visual impressions – unsuccessfully, as can be seen on the third page.

Die Plakatserie beschreibt eine Konversation zwischen einem Mechaniker und mir selbst.

Das erste Plakat zeigt die technische Erklärung des Mechanikers.

Auf dem zweiten Plakat ist zu sehen, wie ich versuche, seine Ausführungen zu verstehen und mit meinen visuellen Eindrücken zu mischen – ohne Erfolg –, wie man auf dem dritten Plakat sieht.

Country

22 | 23

Games with Language
Sprachspiele

< **Natasa Drakula**

Professor:
Eckhard Jung

College:
Hochschule für Künste Bremen

Study Year: **5**

selected by the jury

1→
Warum können wir fernsehen und nicht fernhören? Ein anderer Name für Hörfunk ist Rundfunk. Kann der Rundfunk auch ein Sehfunk sein?
translation impossible

Hörfunk <–> sehfunk
fernhören <–> fernsehen

< Country

Natasa Drakula:

With this I turn to all consumers of words. We're living with language, we live through it and in it, it forms us and we change it. We adapt to it and it adapts to time. Without thinking about its meaning, we use it. We've become consumers of the word through printed books, radio, TV and the Internet. Generally, we hear three times as much as we say. This passive attitude increasingly causes communication problems. A person living in our highly developed industrial society inhales an average of 600 million words in their lifetime. No matter how unnecessary, disturbing, tempting or irritating these words may be.

Herbs and Weeds
With language we create order. Appearances with common characteristics are summarized in superterms. Even feelings can be described. Language can not be separated from thinking. The more clearly we think the more consciously we are able to communicate. Words form our worldviews, and they produce our prejudices. Weeds or pests *(German: »Un-kraut« and »Un-geziefer«)* can be ripped out and stepped on without mercy. With herbs and insects *(German: »Kraut« and »Geziefer«)* we might have more compassion.

»I'm feeling so lousy today«
Half of the words serve social intimacy. Confessing, the writing of poetry, greetings, complaining, chatting, humming, gossiping, comforting. Comfort can be that we express something. As soon as we say, »I'm feeling so lousy today«, we start to feel a little better. Thus, language conjures up the non-existent.

3↓
We don't know from where the ability to speak comes. The origin of most words is unknown to us. There is no direct connection between an uttered sound and its sense. The theories about the origin of language are considered to be wrong. The origin of the word cock and the noise he makes have no connection: cock-a-doodle-do. German cocks go kikeriki, vientnamese go cuc-cu-cu and croatians go kukuriku.

Woher die Sprache und die Fähigkeit zu sprechen kommen, wissen wir nicht. Die Herkunft der meisten Wörter ist unbekannt. Es gibt keine direkte Verbindung zwischen dem Laut und seinem Sinn. Die Theorien über die Sprachentstehung durch Lautmalerei haben sich als falsch erwiesen. So hat die Herkunft des Wortes Hahn wenig gemeinsam mit dem Laut, den er kräht, nämlich kikiriki. Englische Hähne krähen cock-a-doodle-do, vietnamesische cuc-cu-cu, kroatische kukuriku.

Natasa Drakula:

Hiermit wende ich mich an alle Wortkonsumenten. Wir leben mit der Sprache, wir leben durch sie, sie formt uns und wir verändern sie. Wir passen uns an sie an und sie paßt sich der Zeit an. Ohne über ihre Bedeutung nachzudenken, bedienen wir uns ihrer. Durch Buchdruck, Hörfunk, Fernsehen und Internet sind wir zu Konsumenten des Wortes geworden. In der Regel hören wir dreimal so viel wie wir sprechen. Diese passive Haltung zieht zunehmend Kommunikationsprobleme nach sich. Durchschnittlich 600 Millionen Wörter saugt ein Mensch unserer entwickelten →

2→
»Due to construction work on the detour route, the main road has temporarily been opened for traffic.« In Germany, an organizing traffic sign culture is especially developed. In Deutschland ist eine ordnungsstiftende Schilderkultur besonders ausgeprägt.

Gossip and Chat
Language rather rarely serves information. Information is neither the oldest nor the most frequent use of language. Most words apply to entertainment, relating, gossiping or chatting. Sentences like »it may rain today« are found more often in language than informative sentences like »We'll meet at 4 p.m. at Bahnhof Zoo.«

What came first, language or thinking? Do we only have to think clearly to find the right words and be understood by others? Which criteria does good communication meet with?

Industriegesellschaft in seinem Leben ein. Egal wie unwichtig, störend, verführerisch oder irritierend diese Worte sind.

Kraut und Unkraut
Mit Sprache schaffen wir Ordnung. Erscheinungen mit gemeinsamen Merkmalen fassen wir zu Überbegriffen zusammen. Selbst Gefühle können wir beschreiben. Sprache läßt sich nicht vom Denken trennen. Je klarer wir denken, desto bewußter können wir uns mitteilen. Wörter bilden unsere Weltbilder, sie produzieren Vorurteile. Unkraut oder Ungeziefer dürfen wir gnadenlos ausreissen und zertreten. Mit Kraut und Geziefer hätten wir vielleicht mehr Mitgefühl.

»Mir gehts heute so schlecht«
Die Hälfte der Wörter dient dem sozialen Miteinander. Beichten, dichten, grüssen, jammern, quatschen, summen, schwatzen, trösten. Trost kann darin liegen, daß wir etwas aussprechen. Kaum spricht man sich aus: »Mir geht´s heute so schlecht«, geht´s einem gleich ein bißchen besser. So zaubert uns die Sprache das Nichtvorhandene herbei.

Geschwätz und Plaudern
Zur Information dient die Sprache eher selten. Information ist weder die älteste, noch die häufigste Verwendung der Sprache. Die meisten Wörter entfallen auf Unterhaltung, Erzählung, Geschwätz oder Plaudern. Sätze wie: »Es könnte heute regnen«, sind in der Sprache häufiger vertreten als informative Sätze wie: »Wir treffen uns um 16 Uhr am Bahnhof Zoo.« Was war zuerst da, sprechen oder denken? Wie können wir bewußter sprechen? Müssen wir nur klar denken, um die richtigen Worte zu finden und von anderen verstanden zu werden? Welche Kriterien erfüllt eine gute Kommunikation?

ODODRAFIE IS DRIFIAL

4
Sprachen sind reich an Fremdwörtern, die oft nicht genau zu definieren sind. Sie können durch viele treffendere, anschaulichere, heimische Wörter ersetzt werden. So kann das Fremdwort Nuance, je nach Gebrauch mit Abstufung, Tönung, Unterton, Färbung, Farbton, Spur, Hauch, Anflug, Schimmer, Stich, Übergang, Abweichung oder Abart bezeichnet werden.
translation impossible

5
Über Orthographie wird in den meisten Sprachen nur geklagt. In den südslawischen Sprachen wurde schon lange eine Rechtschreibreform durchgeführt. Für jeden Laut gibt es nur einen Buchstaben. Ähnlich ist es auch im Esperanto, der erfolgreichsten Kunstsprache. Hier ein Beispiel der progressiven Orthographie, die schrittweise eingeführt werden soll.
translation impossible

6
Wir sagen oft etwas in einer komplexen und vorgefertigten Sprachform, ohne uns über den eigentlichen Inhalt bewußt zu sein. Wir fallen auf die Nase, machen aus einer Mücke einen Elefanten, nehmen die Beine in die Hand. Noch kurioser wird es, wenn wir die Sprichworte zergliedern: Was haben wir nicht im Schrank? Alle Tassen. Was sagen sich Fuchs und Hase? Gute Nacht. Was machen wir mit Geld? Mit vollen Händen aus dem Fenster werfen. Worauf bringen wir jemanden? Auf die Palme.
sorry, translation impossible

7
Die folgenden Fragen über die Logik der Sprache stellte sich der Wissenschaftstheoretiker Karl Popper:
Die Kaffeemühle mahlt Kaffee – was mahlt die Windmühle?
Die Gefängnisstrafe ist eine Freiheitsstrafe – muß man sie in Freiheit oder im Gefängnis verbringen?
Das Schneckenhaus gehört nicht zwei Schnecken sondern einer; die Zahnbürste dagegen putzt mehr als einen Zahn.
Entspannung hebt die Spannung auf – wie schade, daß Entrüstung nicht die Rüstung beseitigt.
Eine Arbeitspause ist eine Pause zum Nichtarbeiten, eine Atempause jedoch nicht eine Pause zum Nichtatmen.
Ist eine Denkpause eine Pause zum Denken oder zum Nichtdenken?
translation impossible

Außer Raum Dresden ———— ARD
Eierteigwaren
Fleischhaltigeeierteigware ———— Pizza
Erdmöbel
———— coolness
Feierabendbrigade
———— competition sense
———— cleverness
Friedenswacht
Bückware
———— pep
Grilleta
IM
INTERSHOP
Jahresendflügelfigur ———— Engel
die K
———— power
Lichtsignalanlage
Osterfüllartikel
———— know-how
Plaste und Elaste
Sättigungsbeilage

```
Ein     Dorn    im  ehZ
1 Dorn    im   C v er urs 8  W,
 die   V lheit   ist   1  Last  R.
B A T   trinkt   s o gR ne   T,
  im  HR bst   blüh t  die Äst R.
Die   Q  gibt  Milc h.  Die  L 1 Rn Gn
  gar  gR n auf  Dieb R a .
W R  leise    G t, G t  auf  dN  10,
 1  Glas   k r 8 leic h t  N t 2.
Bläst   man  auf  dR  TromPT  Baß
  so  wacKLn al le   WND —
Zum   R nst  wird  oft   1  klein   R  Spaß
  und  al LS  hat   1  ND.
```

Beste ● hende

Spargel ● derkonten

EIN NEGER MIT GAZELLE ZAGT IM REGEN NIE

8
Dieser Satz ist ein Palindrom. Man kann ihn sowohl von hinten als auch von vorne lesen. »Ein Neger mit Gazelle zagt im Regen nie« ist das längste deutsche Palindrom und stammt von Arthur Schopenhauer. Heute hätte er das so nicht erfinden können. Das Wort Neger, das sich von hinten wie Regen liest, hat seine Unschuld verloren
translation impossible

9
Im Deutschen können Wörter zusammengesetzt werden. Die Zusammensetzung von zwei oder mehr Substantiven nach dem Modell Donaudampfschiffahrtsgesellschaftskapitän wird oft belacht und von Deutsch lernenden Ausländern gefürchtet. Einige Beispiele aus der Praxis des Schriftsetzens zeigen die Bedeutungsverschiebung durch eine nicht sinngemäße Trennung: Blumentopferde.
translation impossible

10
Wörter machen die Gesellschaftsverhältnisse deutlich, wie auch das Beispiel Ost- und Westdeutschland zeigt. Welche Begriffe hatten die Westdeutschen für Feierabendbrigade, Bückware, Sättigungsbeilage? Was sagten die Ostdeutschen für Know-how, clever, Power und Management? ARD hieß Außer-Raum-Dresden, weil man »im Tal der Ahnungslosen« das westdeutsche Fernsehprogramm nicht empfangen konnte.
translation impossible

Morbid Beauty

Kelly Stevens

Professor:
Katie Salen

College:
The University of Texas at Austin

Study Year: 3

selected by the jury

Country

Kelly Stevens:

My work addresses the manifestation of morbid beauty in the female ream, and focuses on five areas which reference have been most affected by a (postmodern) morbid aesthetic: technology, appropriation, dark heroines, artificial nature and eras of decadence.

Meine Arbeit behandelt die Manifestation morbider Schönheit im Reich der Weiblichkeit und konzentriert sich auf fünf Bereiche, die am stärksten von einer (postmodernen) morbiden Ästhetik beeinflußt wurden: Technologie, Aneignung, dunkle Heldinnen, künstliche Natur und dekadente Zeitalter.

At the Station
Am Bahnhof

Kiyo Matsumoto

College:
Minneapolis College of Art and Design

Study Year: **4**

selected by the jury

Country

28

Paint it Yourself

Miriam Kaddoura

Professor:
Leila Musfy

College:
American University
of Beirut

Study Year: 3

chosen by contributing editor
Leila Musfy

Country

Sabine Kobel:

»'60 '61 '62« is a book about the sixties. The research for this book mainly consisted in »rummaging« through my parents' house, the family album, drawers, bookshelves and at flea markets. Many of the photographs I used were taken from the family album, but I also took pictures of objects that my parents have kept from the sixties (e.g. the braid my mother had cut off during the sixties and my father's first tape recorder).

Book about the 60's
Buch über die 60er Jahre

Sabine Kobel

Professor:
Hans-Georg Pospischil

College:
Akademie der bildenden Künste Stuttgart

Study Year: 5

selected by the jury

Sabine Kobel:

»'60 '61 '62« ist ein Buch über die Sechziger Jahre. Die Recherche zu diesem Buch bestand zum großen Teil aus »Wühlen« – dem Stöbern im Haus meiner Eltern, im Familienalbum, in Schubladen, Bücherregalen und auf dem Flohmarkt.

Die verwendeten Fotografien stammen zum Teil aus dem Familienalbum, zum Teil habe ich aber auch Gegenstände abfotografiert, die meine Eltern seit den Sechziger Jahren aufbewahrt haben (z.B. den Zopf den sich meine Mutter in den Sechzigern abschneiden ließ oder das erste Tonbandgerät meines Vaters).

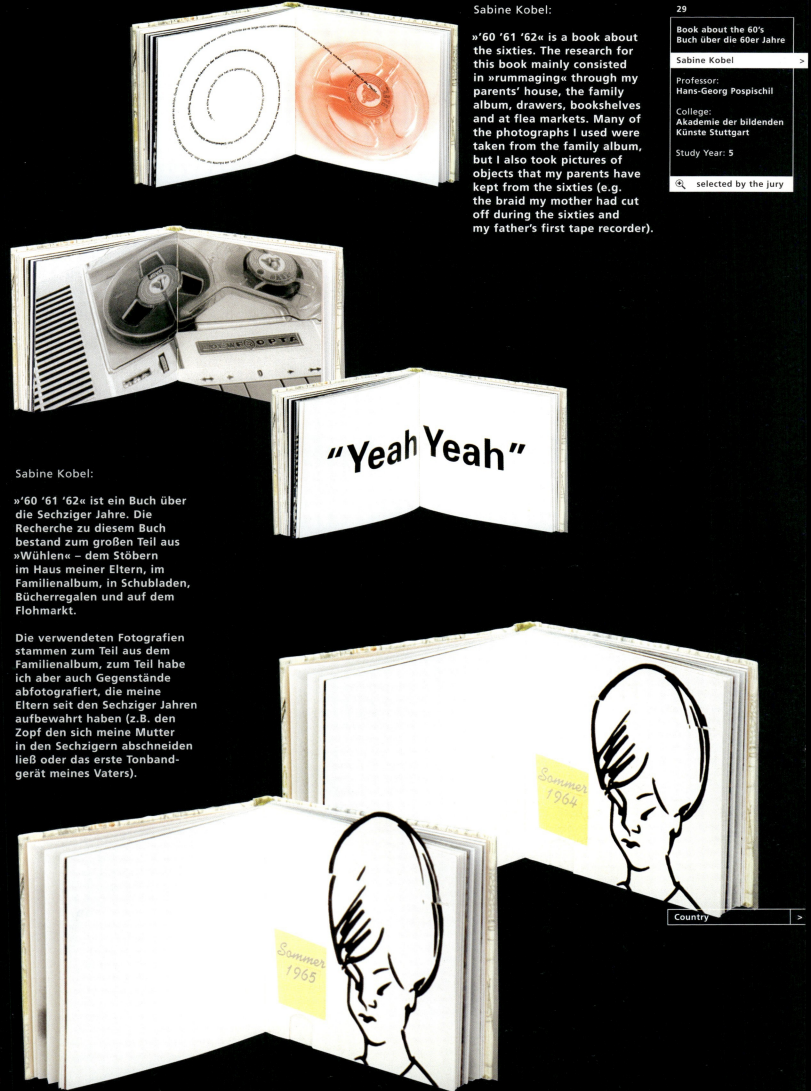

Country

Package
Verpacken

< **Esmeralda Schürch**

Professor:
Polly Bertram

College:
Schule für Gestaltung Zürich

🔍 selected by the jury

< Country

Polly Bertram:

Every packaging that is bought over and again – including that from the supermarket – will finally become established in a household. The goal of the work was the occupation with packaging for its own sake, not a debate about the communication of its content. The work examines the geometric structure of packaging based on the cube, cylinder and tube types, its coloration in the environment of its use and possibilities for design influences on their perception as volumes. The means are found images and patterns of varying origin in different techniques of realization.

Jede wieder und wieder gekaufte Packung, auch die aus dem Supermarkt, bürgert sich schlußendlich in einem Haushalt ein. Ziel der Arbeit war eine Beschäftigung mit der Verpackung um ihrer selbst willen, nicht eine Auseinandersetzung mit der Vermittlung deren Inhalts. Gestalterisch untersucht die Arbeit anhand von Grundtypen Kubus, Zylinder und Tube das geometrische Gerüst von Verpackungen, deren Farbigkeit im Umfeld ihrer Verwendung und mögliche gestalterische Einflußmöglichkeiten auf deren Wahrnehmung als Körper. Mittel dazu sind vorgefundene Bilder und Muster unterschiedlicher Herkunft in verschiedenen Umsetzungstechniken.

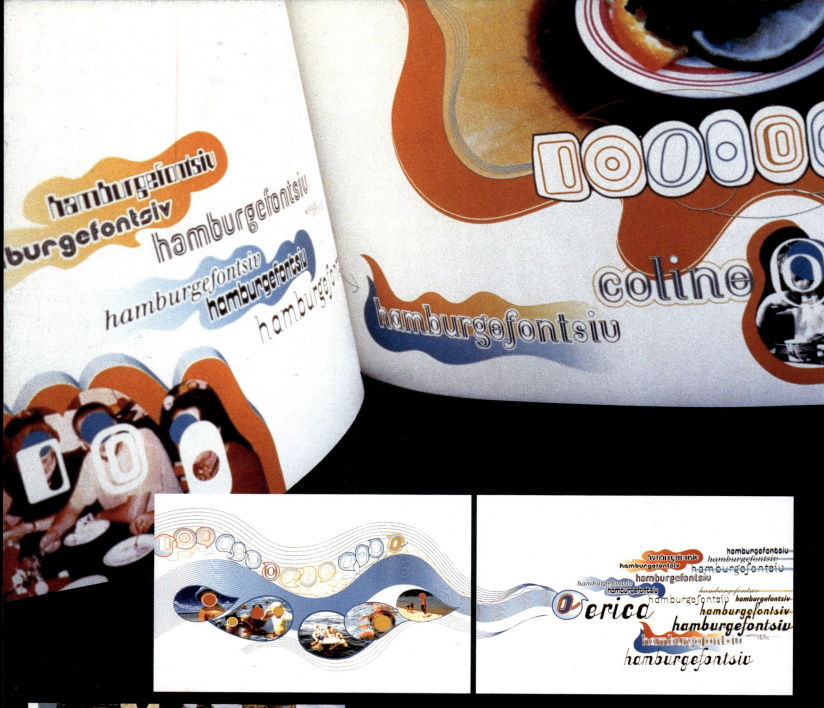

is a type family that reflects a playful, alternative rationale for formulating typographic form. Using »genetics« as the basic principle to derive the typefaces, Family Affair was created by applying the basic principles of genetics to Font Design: Two original fonts »marry« and »breed« to produce a 3rd font, who in turn marry and produce offspring. The result is a family that can be traced over several generations.

The system used to create Family Affair, begins with 2 original »parents« selected according to placement in the alphabet. Each letter marries the next in order: For instance, A, arbitrarily selected as »Arnold Boecklin«, »marries« B, »Bureau Agency«. These 2 fonts »breed« by combining dominant characteristics, subjectively selected by the designer, to produce an offspring typeface. The family then perpetuates over 4-5 generations to result in Family Affair. The final representation of the project was in the form of a family Album and family tree.

ist eine Schrifttypenfamilie, die einen spielerischen, alternativen Ansatz für die Formulierung typographischer Form vertritt. Family Affair wurde durch Anwendung von Grundprinzipien der »Genetik« für die Ableitung der Schriften, geschaffen: zwei Schriften »heiraten« und »vermehren sich«, um eine 3D-Schrift zu erzeugen, die wiederum heiratet und Nachkommen erzeugt. Das Ergebnis ist eine Familie, die sich über mehrere Generationen zurückverfolgen läßt.

Das System, mit dem Family Affair erzeugt wurde, beginnt mit 2 »Eltern«, die entsprechend ihrer Plazierung im Alphabet ausgewählt wurden. Jeder Buchstabe heiratet den ihm folgenden. Zum Beispiel »heiratet« A, das beliebig als »Arnold Böcklin« gewählt wurde, B, »Bureau Agency«. Die beiden Schriften »vermehren sich« durch die Kombination dominanter Eigenschaften, die vom Designer subjektiv ausgesucht wurden, um eine Nachkommen-Schrift zu erzeugen. Die Familie pflanzt sich dann über 4-5 Generationen hin fort und endet in Family Affair. Die letzte Darstellung des Projekts fand in Form eines Familien-Albums und Stammbaums statt.

Family Affair
Familienangelegenheit

Andrea Tinnes >

Professor:
Ed Fella
Jeff Keedy
Lorraine Wild

College:
California Institute
of Arts

Study Year: 1

chosen by
contributing editor
Louise Sandhaus

Country >

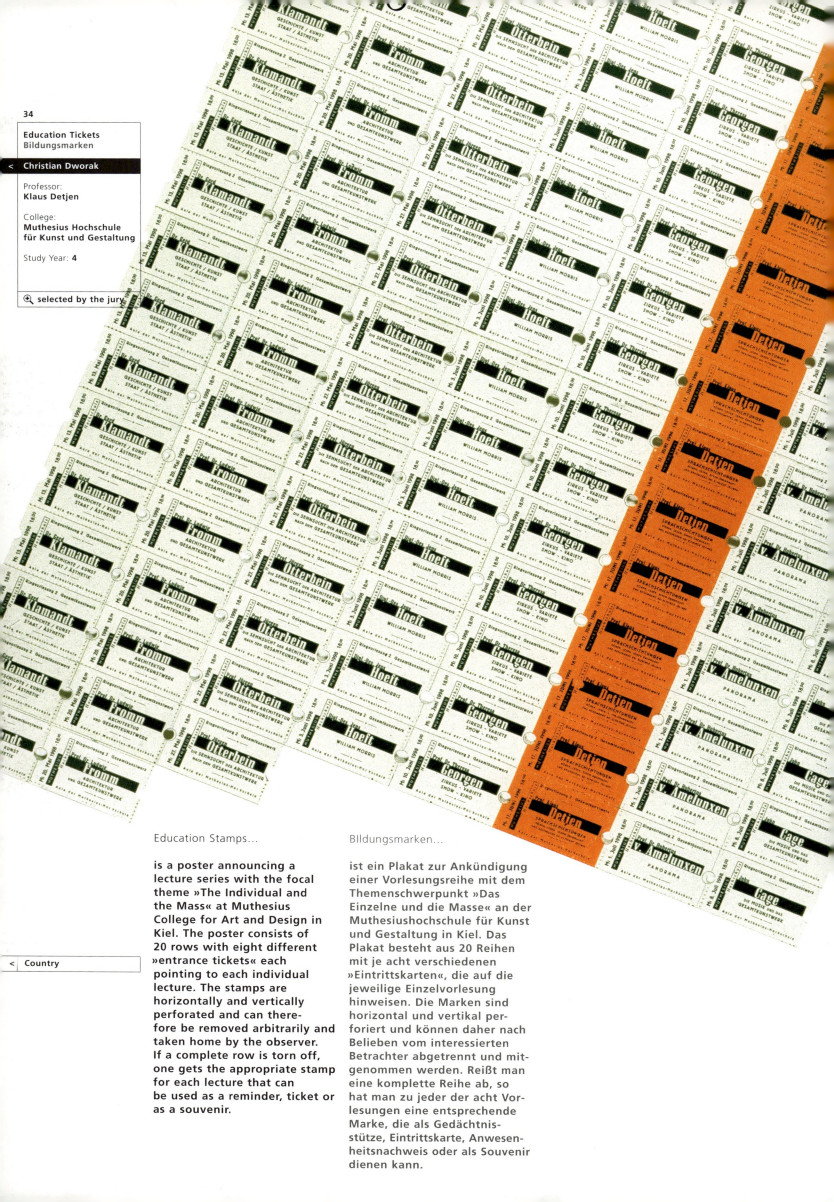

34

Education Tickets
Bildungsmarken

< Christian Dworak

Professor:
Klaus Detjen

College:
Muthesius Hochschule
für Kunst und Gestaltung

Study Year: 4

selected by the jury

< Country

Education Stamps…

is a poster announcing a lecture series with the focal theme »The Individual and the Mass« at Muthesius College for Art and Design in Kiel. The poster consists of 20 rows with eight different »entrance tickets« each pointing to each individual lecture. The stamps are horizontally and vertically perforated and can therefore be removed arbitrarily and taken home by the observer. If a complete row is torn off, one gets the appropriate stamp for each lecture that can be used as a reminder, ticket or as a souvenir.

Bildungsmarken…

ist ein Plakat zur Ankündigung einer Vorlesungsreihe mit dem Themenschwerpunkt »Das Einzelne und die Masse« an der Muthesiushochschule für Kunst und Gestaltung in Kiel. Das Plakat besteht aus 20 Reihen mit je acht verschiedenen »Eintrittskarten«, die auf die jeweilige Einzelvorlesung hinweisen. Die Marken sind horizontal und vertikal perforiert und können daher nach Belieben vom interessierten Betrachter abgetrennt und mitgenommen werden. Reißt man eine komplette Reihe ab, so hat man zu jeder der acht Vorlesungen eine entsprechende Marke, die als Gedächtnisstütze, Eintrittskarte, Anwesenheitsnachweis oder als Souvenir dienen kann.

Hotel for Fine Arts
Hotel für bildende Künste

At Hamburg University for Fine Arts, a summer festival was held under the motto »Hotel for Fine Arts«. Students, friends, relatives and especially students from other universities were invited to pass a weekend in the university.

Unter dem Motto »Hotel für bildende Künste« wurde in der Hochschule für bildende Künste in Hamburg ein Sommerfest veranstaltet. Studierende der HfK, Freunde, Bekannte und insbesondere Studierende anderer Hochschulen waren eingeladen, in der Hochschule ein Wochenende zu verbringen.

35

Hotel for Fine Arts
Hotel für bildende Künste

Christiane Bruckmann

Professor:
Hans Andree

College:
Hochschule für Bildende Künste Hamburg

Study Year: **6**

selected by the jury

Country

Flight KE 007

Maike Freiberg +
Indra Häußler +
Maryam Miremadi

Professor:
Sandra Hoffmann

College:
Fachhochschule
Darmstadt

Study Year: 4

selected by the jury

On August 31, 1983 a South Korean Boeing 747 (flight number KE007) entered Russian airspace and was shot down by a Soviet interceptor above the island of Sakhalin.

The research reports of the International Civil Aviation Organization in Montreal served as the basis for this work dealing with the tragedy.

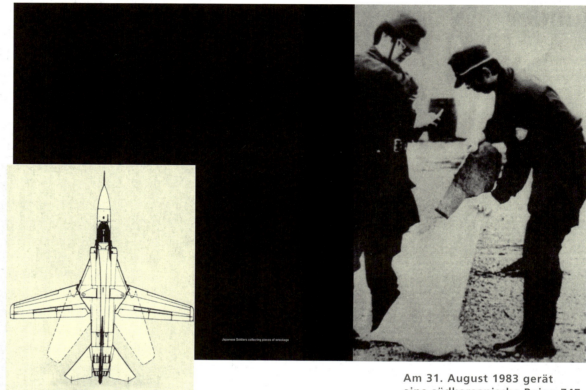

Am 31. August 1983 gerät eine südkoreanische Boing 747 (Flugnummer KE007) in russischen Luftraum und wird von einem sowjetischen Abfangjäger über der Insel Sachalin angeschossen.

Grundlage der Arbeit, die sich mit der Geschichte dieser Tragödie beschäftigt, sind die Untersuchungsberichte der International Civil Aviation Organization, Montreal.

Country

Homepage of
the School of Design,
Nepean, Sydney

Tobias Grime
Stanley Yip

Professor:
Robyn Stacey

College:
School of Design
UWS, Nepean,
Sydney

chosen by
contributing editor
Robyn Stacey

complete work
on the CD-ROM

Robyn Stacey:

The school web site was designed specifically to promote the school to potential undergraduate and postgraduate students.

Designing for cyberspace the question arose how is a distinctive experience possible in this kind of environment that lacks history, materiality, and has no fixed form.

We addressed this question of identity by grounding the web site design in the physical structure of the school itself. The distinctive architectural features of the school - the archway and bright colours were used to »brand« the site and became the dominant interface design.

Robyn Stacey:

Die Homepage wurde vor allem mit dem Ziel erstellt, die Hochschule potentiellen Studenten näher zu bringen.

Beim Design für den Cyberspace stellt sich vor allem die Frage, wie in dieser Umgebung ohne Geschichte, Materialität und feste Form eine deutliche Erfahrung möglich wird. Wir haben diese Identitätsfrage dahingehend gelöst, das Webdesign auf der physischen Struktur der Schule zu begründen. Die deutlichen architektonischen Merkmale der Schule – der Bogen und die leuchtenden Farben – wurden für das Branding der Site eingesetzt und wurden zum dominierenden Interface-Design.

EVERYONE IS A DESIGNER

Country

5. Internationale Designkonferenz: TYPO BERLIN 2000
13.–15. April 2000

Früh anmelden lohnt sich:

Subskriptionspreis bis 31.12.1999:
DM 590,– (Studenten DM 250,–)

Vom 01.01.2000 bis 27.02.2000:
DM 890,– (Studenten DM 350,–)

ab 28.02.2000:
DM 1200,– (Studenten DM 450,–)

Prominente Sprecher aus
Design
Architektur
Kunst
Drei Bühnen
Ausstellungen
Messe
Buffet
Inspiration
Kontakte
Unterhaltung
Spaß

Seit 5 Jahren veranstaltet FontShop den Designkongreß TYPO BERLIN im Haus der Kulturen der Welt (»Schwangere Auster«). Die Veranstaltung gilt als der bedeutendste Treff der europäischen Designszene. Zum 5. Mal treffen sich für drei Tage über 1500 Grafikdesigner und Kommunikationsexperten, um Themen der digitalen visuellen Kommunikation zu erörtern. Das Streitobjekt: Style. Ein anregendes Rahmenprogramm rundet die Veranstaltung ab.

FontShop Berlin, Bergmannstraße 102, 10961 Berlin, Infotelefon (0 30) 69 58 95
FontShop: Handel und Dienstleistungen für Typografie und Design

40 | 41

Theatre Posters
Theaterplakate

Agnes Rozanska-Haager

Professor:
Eckhard Jung

College:
Hochschule für Künste Bremen

selected by the jury

↑1

↓2
↓4

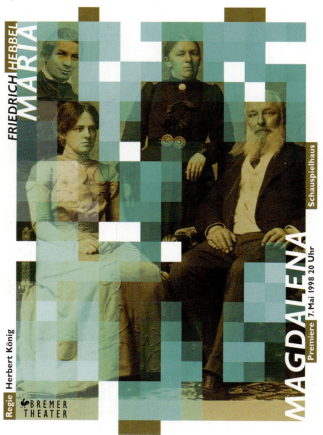
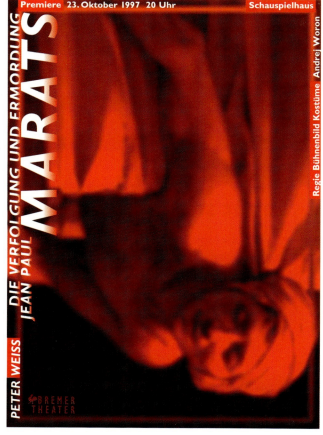

< Country

1
Fat men in skirts
Fette Männer im Rock
A fancy upper-class woman and her strange son are the only survivors of an airplane crash and strand on a lonely island. To surive they start to eat the bodies of the other passengers (...)
Eine mondäne Upper-Class Frau und ihr seltsamer Sohn überleben als einzige einen Flugzeugabsturz und stranden irgendwo auf einer einsamen Insel. Um zu überleben werden die Leichen der Flugzeugpassagiere verspeist (...)

2
Maria Magdalena
Klara, the daughter of Anton the carpenter, is pregnant by Leonhard, who she does not love. When her brother Karl is suspected of being a thief, he drops her. The breakdown of the family and the shame in society make the insecure father insist, with increasing desperation, on his moral ideas.
Klara, die Tochter des Tischlers Anton, ist schwanger von Leonhard, den sie nicht liebt. Er läßt Klara fallen, als deren Bruder Karl als Dieb verdächtigt wird. Der Zusammenbruch der Familie und die gesellschaftliche Schande lassen den verunsicherten Vater immer verzweifelter auf seinen Moralvorstellungen beharren.

3
La Chute
In her pieces »Frauenballett« (women's ballet) and »Heiße Luft« (hot air) choreographer Susanne Linke deals with fabric as a theme and basic material, reducing textiles to threads: the thread that leads through life, the thread one can loose, the thread in which we are entangled, the thread that rips and binds.
In ihren Stücken »Frauenballett« und »Heiße Luft« beschäftigt sich die Choreographin Susanne Linke mit dem Thema und Grundmaterial Stoff und reduziert das Gewebe auf den Faden: Der Faden, der durchs Leben führt, den man verliert, in dem wir verstrickt sind, der reißt, der einen bindet.

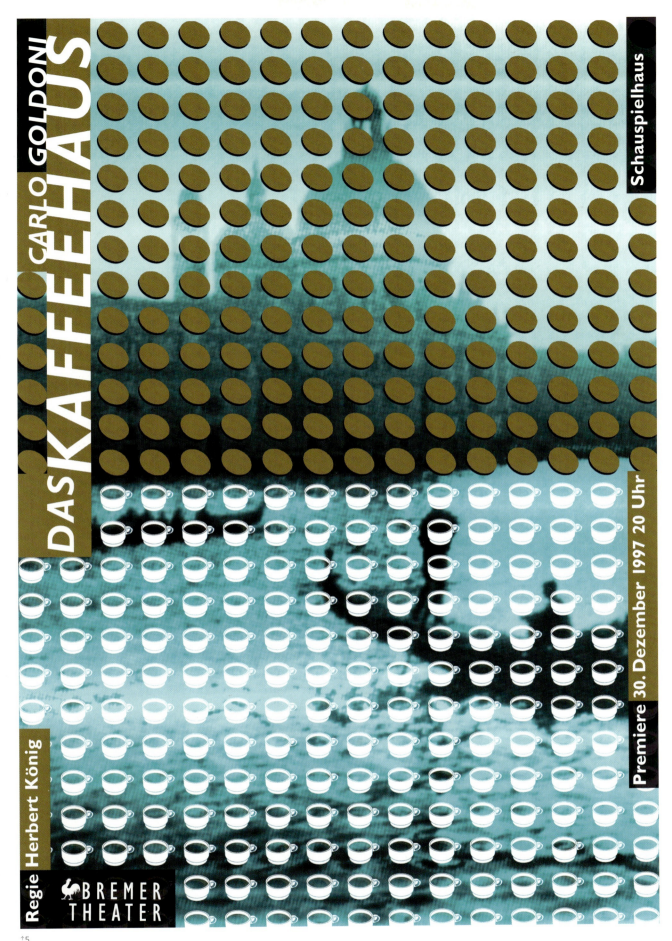

4
The prosecution and murder
of Jean-Paul Marats
Die Verfolgung und Ermordung
Jean Paul Marats
In the Charenton psychiatric clinic the
Marquis de Sade, who is locked up within,
lets the inmates perform a play about
the life of Jean-Paul Marat. De Sade is the
hedonistic, anarchist defender of individual
freedom. Marat, however, is an active
politician, an idealist, and an ideologist as
well, who knows about the necessity
of a collective social and socially-relevant
solution even though it might cost the blood
of the individual.
In der psychiatrischen Heilanstalt Charenton
läßt der dort eingesperrte Marquis de
Sade von den Insassen ein Theaterstück
über das Leben des Jean-Paul Marat
aufführen. De Sade ist der genußsüchtige,
anarchistische Verteidiger der individuellen
Freiheit. Marat dagegen ist aktiver
Politiker, Idealist und Ideologe, der
um die Notwendigkeit einer kollektiven,
gesellschaftlichen und sozialen Lösung
weiß – auch wenn sie das Blut des
Einzelnen kosten sollte.

5
The Coffee House
Das Kaffehaus
In a small square in Venice, vice and virtue
live side by side. There, in an uneven
neighborhood, the coffee house of the
virtuous Ridolfo and the gambling
house of the unscrupulous profiteer
Pandolfo stand next to one another. Torn
between the two is Eugenio, a young
businessman, because he has been taken
with a passion for gambling (...)
Auf einem kleinen Platz in Venedig
wohnen das Laster und die Tugend Tür an
Tür. In ungleicher Nachbarschaft stehen
dort das Kaffeehaus des redlichen Ridolfo
und das Spielhaus des skrupellosen
Geschäftemachers Pandolfo. Zwischen
beiden hin- und hergerissen ist Eugenio,
ein junger Kaufmann, denn die
Spielleidenschaft hat ihn gepackt (...)

Kerstin Deindörfer
Silke Kemnitz:

»The garden represents the synchronicity of nature and culture.« This quote by Dieter Kienast describes a central assertion of garden history. We attempted a humorous interpretation in view of today's computer age.

The G@rden
Der G@rten

< Silke Kemnitz +
Kerstin Deindörfer

Professor:
Erwin Grießel

College:
Fachhochschule Würzburg

Study Year: 5

selected by the jury

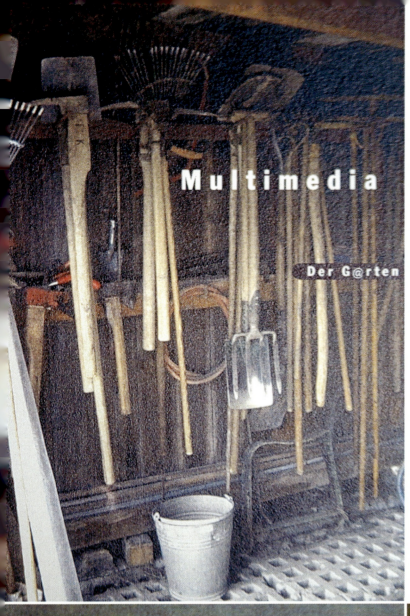

Kerstin Deindörfer
Silke Kemnitz:

»Der Garten stellt die Gleichzeitigkeit von Natur und Kultur dar.« Dieses Zitat von Dieter Kienast beschreibt eine zentrale Aussage der Gartengeschichte. In Bezug auf das heutige Computerzeitalter haben wir eine humorvolle Interpretation versucht.

44

Albert Einstein

< Erkut Terliksiz

Professor:
Esen Karol

College:
Mimar Sinan University
Istanbul

chosen by
contributing editor
Sadik Karamustafa

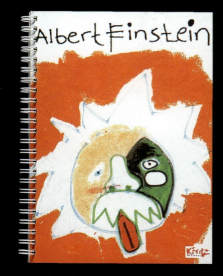

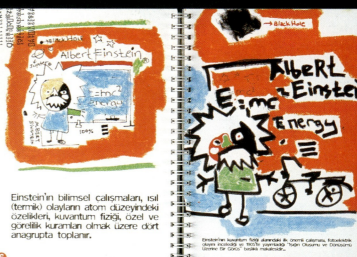

< Country

Bianca Wessalowski:

The object, a plasticope, contains ten images with quotes by Stephen Hawking. The basic idea is that different stories happen at different places and at different times.

Das Objekt, ein Plastikop, enthält zehn Bilder mit Zitaten von Stephen Hawking. Die Grundidee ist, daß unterschiedliche Geschichten an unterschiedlichen Orten zu unterschiedlichen Zeiten geschehen.

1 The special relativity theory describes how objects move through space and time.

2 The earth is round and moves around the sun.

3 Why is the density of the universe so close to the critical point?

45

The Universe is expanding
Das Universum expandiert

Bianca Wessalowski

Professor:
Bernd Bexte

College:
Hochschule für Künste Bremen

Study Year: **4**

selected by the jury

1↓

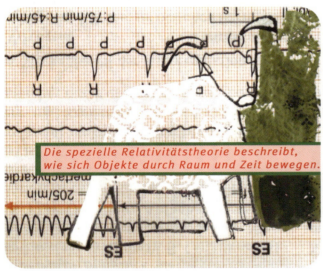

2↓

←3

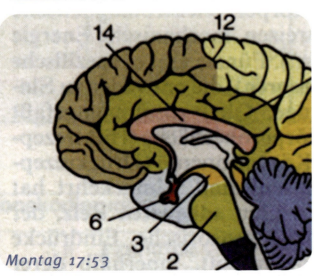

Country

Poster for a German/French cultural event in Dortmund, Germany

46

German-French Culture Days
Deutsch-Französische Kulturtage

< **Jörg Hemker**

Professor:
Prof. Ziegenfeuter
Prof. Schrader

College:
Fachhochschule Dortmund

Study Year: **5**

selected by the jury

< Country

deutsch-französische Kulturtage der Stadt Dortmund
4.–10. September 1998

47

Poster: konkret

**Friederike Lambers +
Dorthe Meinhardt**

Professor:
Fritz Haase

College:
Hochschule für Künste Bremen

Study Year: **5**

selected by the jury

Poster for a lecture of Philip Rosenthal at the college of Fine Arts in Bremen, Germany.

The theme of the lecture was concrete poetry, concrete art, concrete music and design.

Plakat für eine Vorlesung von Philip Rosenthal an der Hochschule für Künste Bremen.

Unter dem Titel »konkret« wurde über konkrete Poesie, konkrete Kunst, konkrete Musik und Design gesprochen.

Country

48

Childhood is not a child's game
Kindheit ist kein Kinderspiel

Sandra Dörfler

Professor:
Gunter Rambow

College:
Hochschule für Gestaltung Karlsruhe

Study Year: 5

selected by the jury

Country

1-3 Childhood is no Child's Game

1   He makes mess in his pants again
     (Mummy has stress at work)

2   Nothing can be seen
     (The spots are on the back)

3   She's afraid of taking a shower
     (Uncle's little princess)

49

Posters for amnesty international

Jan Haux >

Professor:
Gunter Rambow

College:
Hochschule für Gestaltung Karlsruhe

Study Year: **3**

selected by the jury

Posters for the human rights organisation »amnesty international«

Plakate für die Menschenrechtsorganisation »amnesty international«

Country >

Elena Isaeva:

The catalogue of our college shows the figurative story about studied subjects and particular activities of the students.

The »book in the book« contains student works which have been published.

Das Jahrbuch unserer Hochschule stellt in anschaulicher Art und Weise die Studieninhalte und besonderen Aktivitäten der Studierenden dar.

Das »Buch im Buch« zeigt Arbeiten, die veröffentlicht worden sind.

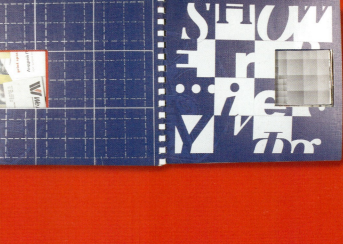

50 | 51

**Brochure of the college
Selbstdarstellung der Hochschule**

Elena Isaeva >

Professor:
Boris Trofimov

College:
High Academy School of Graphic Design, Moscow

🔍 selected by the jury

Country >

52 | 53

Me too in Arcadia
Auch ich in Arkadien

< **Dorothee Stickling**

Professor:
Frieder Grindler

College:
Fachhochschule Würzburg

Study Year: **5**

🔍 selected by the jury

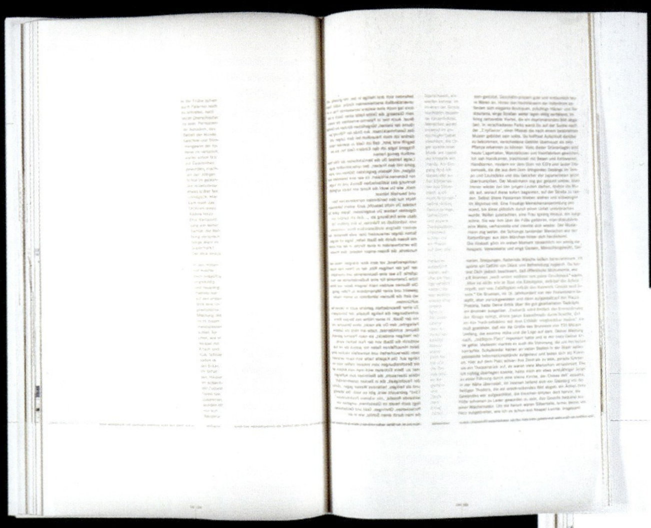

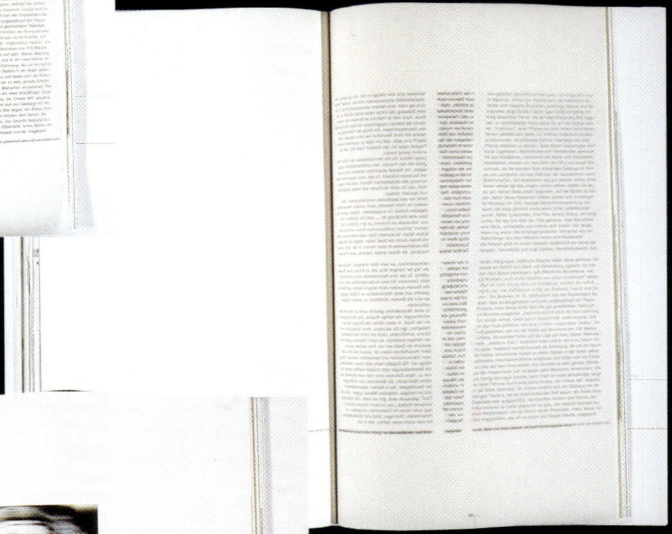

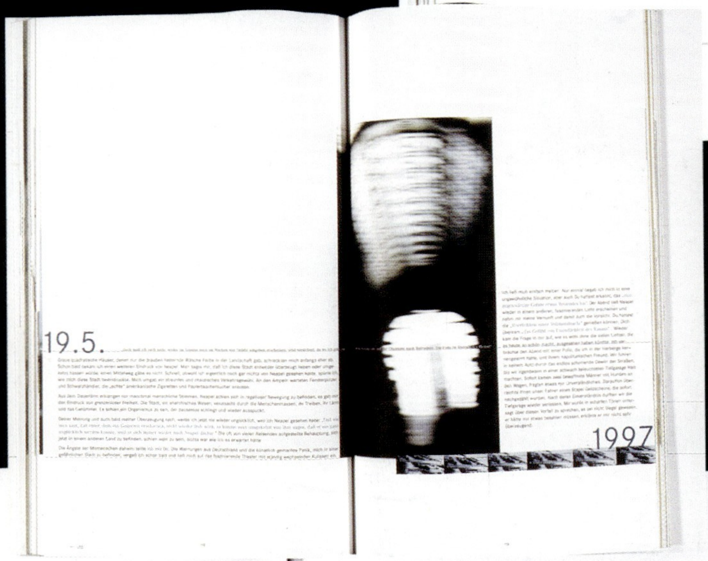

< Country

Dorothee Stickling:

The emotional and very subjective image described by Johann Wolfgang von Goethe in his book »An Italian Journey« gave me the impulse to take my own journey and to follow in Goethe's footsteps.

Goethe was my imaginary travel companion to whom I would tell in a book how I fared along the route. My travel journal describes every-day life, the normal, and not the sublime and special. Thus, Goethe became my confidant during this journey to whom I could tell all.

I compared my own personal impressions of the 20th century with those of the past, the 18th century. I was astonished how many of the statements made by Goethe 200 years ago still apply today. Often, the people I encountered on my journey thought in ways very similar to those described by Goethe.

My book is structured in 7 chapters, as is the »Italian Journey«: I began my drive on the 45th parallel and then moved on to the southernmost point of the journey, the 38th parallel, progressing with each chapter.

Once in Sicily, Goethe had had enough. I felt the same way and only wanted to get home as quickly as possible.

Das emotionale und sehr subjektive Bild, das Johann Wolfgang von Goethe in seinem Buch »Italienische Reise« beschreibt, gab mir den Impuls, eine eigene Reise zu unternehmen und den Spuren Goethes zu folgen.

Goethe war dabei mein imaginärer Reisepartner, dem ich in meinem Buch erzähle, wie es mir auf seiner Reiseroute ergangen ist. Mein Reisebericht beschreibt dabei den Alltag, das Normale und nicht das Erhabene und Besondere. So wurde Goethe im Lauf der Reise mein Vertrauter, dem ich alles schildern konnte.

Meine eigenen persönlichen Eindrücke am Ende des 20. Jahrhunderts habe ich mit denen der Vergangenheit, des 18. Jahrhunderts verglichen. Erstaunlich war, daß viele Aussagen, die Goethe vor 200 Jahren gemacht hat, heute immer noch aktuell sind.

Oft dachten die Menschen, die ich getroffen habe, ganz ähnlich wie die, von denen Goethe berichtet.

Wie die »Italienische Reise« ist mein Buch in sieben Kapitel unterteilt: Ich habe meine Fahrt auf dem 45. Breitengrad begonnen und bin dann kapitelweise bis zum 38. Grad gewandert – dem südlichsten Punkt der Reise.

In Sizilien angekommen hatte Goethe keine Lust mehr. So ging's mir dort auch, ich wollte nur noch schnell nach Hause.

↑1

1-4 TV-Trailer
(also on the CD-ROM)
*TV-Trailer
(auch auf der CD-ROM)*
5 Program Announcement
Programmankündigung

54 | 55

| canal blond |
| < **Bettina Bruder** |

Professor:
Frieder Grindler

College:
Fachhochschule Würzburg

Study Year: **6**

⊕ selected by the jury

◉ also on the CD-ROM

←5→

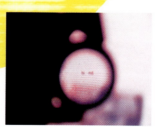 

↑3

< Country

↓4

Bettina Bruder:

»canal blond« is thus far only a fictitious station that broadcasts videos and contributions from its viewers in the area of Cologne. The professional stations are counterbalanced by a more personal TV where communication with and between the viewers is at the center of attention.

Target group:
The station is generally targeted at everybody. There is no restricted target group. »blond« represents people who wear glasses, people who drink milk, vegetarians, bowlegged people, shortsighted people, people with dentures, overweight people...

The program:
The program is shown as a TV happening that takes place once a month on a »blond day«. There are no restrictions with respect to themes, but there are moral and ethical principles that are followed. The contributions can have a maximum length of 24 minutes. Except for the commercials advertising the station itself, there are no programming contributions by the station and there are no commercials.

The name:
»blond« is a call for tolerance and openness, »blond« opposes thinking in narrow categories, the name works with insecurity, irrationality and curiosity. The viewer tries to create his or her own image of how a blond TV station could be. It's fun to imagine watching blond on blond day and to think and feel blond. The general stereotype – blond is dumb, blond is randy – is consciously played with. The station is called »blond« just for spite. This is how the station achieves its freedom. In the »blond« logo, the letter »o« is left out and should be added by the viewer.

Visual conception:
The appearance of »canal blond« is flexible. It intends to create a setting for diverse contributions. A uniform presentation is achieved by the continuity of different stylistic means: lines, focus/blur, interruptions, typography...

Only images photographed from the monitor or single frames from the digital video clips are used as image material in the print area.

↑2

Bettina Bruder:

»canal blond« ist bislang noch ein fiktiver Fernsehsender, der im Raum Köln nur Videos und Beiträge von seinen Zuschauern sendet. Den professionellen Fernsehsendern wird ein persönliches Fernsehen entgegengesetzt, bei dem die Kommunikation mit und zwischen den Zuschauern im Mittelpunkt steht.

Die Zielgruppe
Der Sender richtet sich grundsätzlich an jeden. Eine begrenzte Zielgruppe gibt es nicht. »blond« steht stellvertretend für Brillenträger, Milchtrinker, Vegetarier, O-Beiner, Kurzsichtige, Gebißträger, Übergewichtige...

Das Programm
Das Programm wird als TV-Happening gezeigt, das einmal im Monat am blondtag stattfindet. Es gibt keine Einschränkungen bezüglich der Themen, aber moralische und ethische Grundsätze. Die Beiträge können maximal 24 Minuten lang sein. Außer den Trailern zur Eigenwerbung und zur Wiedererkennung gibt es keine Eigenbeiträge des Senders und keine Werbung.

Die Namensfindung
»blond« ist ein Aufruf zu Toleranz und Offenheit, »blond« steht gegen Schubladendenken, der Name arbeitet mit Verunsicherung, Irritation und Neugier. Der Betrachter versucht, sich sein eigenes Bild zu auszumalen, wie ein blonder Fernsehsender sein könnte. Es macht Spaß, sich vorzustellen, am blondtag blond zu sehen und überhaupt blond zu denken und zu fühlen. Mit den allgemein verbreiteten Vorurteilen blond ist blöd, blond ist geil... wird bewußt gespielt. Der Sender heißt »blond« gerade zum Trotz. Dadurch erreicht der Sender seine Freiheit.

Im Logo »blond« kommt der Buchstabe »o« nicht vor, die Lücke soll vom Betrachter ergänzt werden.

visuelle Konzeption
Das Erscheinungsbild von »canal blond« ist flexibel. Es soll einen Rahmen für unterschiedlichste Beiträge schaffen. Ein einheitlicher Auftritt wird durch die Kontinuität von verschiedenen Stilmitteln erreicht: Linien, Schärfe/Unschärfe, Störungen, Typografie...

Als Bildmaterial im Print-Bereich werden ausschließlich vom Monitor abfotografierte Bilder oder Einzelframes aus den digitalen Videoclips verwendet.

← 6 *Sticker*
  Aufkleber

→ 7 *Hair Curl Mailing*
  Lockenwickler-Mailing

→→ 8 *Business Cards*
  Visitenkarten

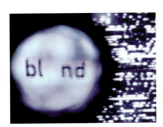

Christiane Bruckmann:

The pool at Stadtpark Lake is to receive a new image. Before, opinion polls and information events were held. Additionally, a competition for architects or investors was to be held. A symbol was to be developed for the moderation of this undertaking.

The symbol shows an oval »with a neck«, the ground plan of Stadtpark Lake with the small, oval »love island«.

Ein neues Gesicht für das STADTPARKBAD?

58

**New Face for the pool at Stadtpark Lake
Ein neues Gesicht für das Stadtparkbad**

< **Christiane Bruckmann**

Professor:
Hans Andree

College:
Hochschule für bildende Künste Hamburg

Study Year: **6**

selected by the jury

Öffentliche Informationsveranstaltung zur zukünftigen Entwicklung der Stadtparkbades
4. Sept. 1997, 18 Uhr
Heinrich Hertz Schule, Aula
Grasweg 72-76, 22303 Hamburg
Umweltbehörde Hamburg und PPL-Planungsgruppe Professor Laage

Christiane Bruckmann:

Das Schwimmbad am Stadtparksee soll ein neues Image bekommen. Im Vorfeld liefen Bügerbefragungen und Informationsveranstaltungen. Auch ein architektonischer und ein Investorenwettbewerb wurden ausgeschrieben. Für die Moderation dieses Vorhabens sollte ein Zeichen entwickelt werden.

Das Zeichen zeigt ein Oval »mit Hals« – den Grundriss des Stadtparksees – mit der kleinen ovalen Liebesinsel.

 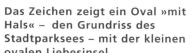 

< Country

»Das Planetensystem« ist ein interaktives Projekt zum Semesterthema Visuelle Daten.

Die neun bekannten Planeten Merkur, Venus, Mars, Erde, Jupiter, Saturn, Uranus, Neptun und Pluto werden in ihren Eigenschaften hinsichtlich Entfernung, Durchmesser, Temperatur, Umlaufzeit, Bahngeschwindigkeit, Entweichungsgeschwindigkeit, Helligkeit und Satellitenanzahl dargestellt und durch Diagramme sowie Filme veranschaulicht.

Anja Denz:

»The Planetary System« is an interactive project on the theme of the semester, visual data.

The nine planets Mercury, Venus, Mars, Earth, Jupiter, Saturn, Uranus, Neptune and Pluto are presented in their characteristics with regard to distance, diameter, temperature, period of revolution, orbital speed, escape velocity, luminosity and number of satellites and are made clear through diagrams and films.

0	Merkur
0	Venus
1	Erde
2	Mars
16	Jupiter
20	Saturn
15	Uranus
2	Neptun
1	Pluto

Alle Neun

The Planetary System
Das Planetensystem

Anja Denz

Professor:
Michael Klar

College:
Hochschule der Künste Berlin

Study Year: 6

selected by the jury

complete work on the CD-ROM

Country >

60

Cult Shoes
Kultschuhe

< **Marta Daul +
Ingrid Klinger**

Professor:
Fritz Haase

College:
**Hochschule für Künste
Bremen**

Study Year: **4**

🔍 selected by the jury

< Country

Free Photographs
Freie Fotografien

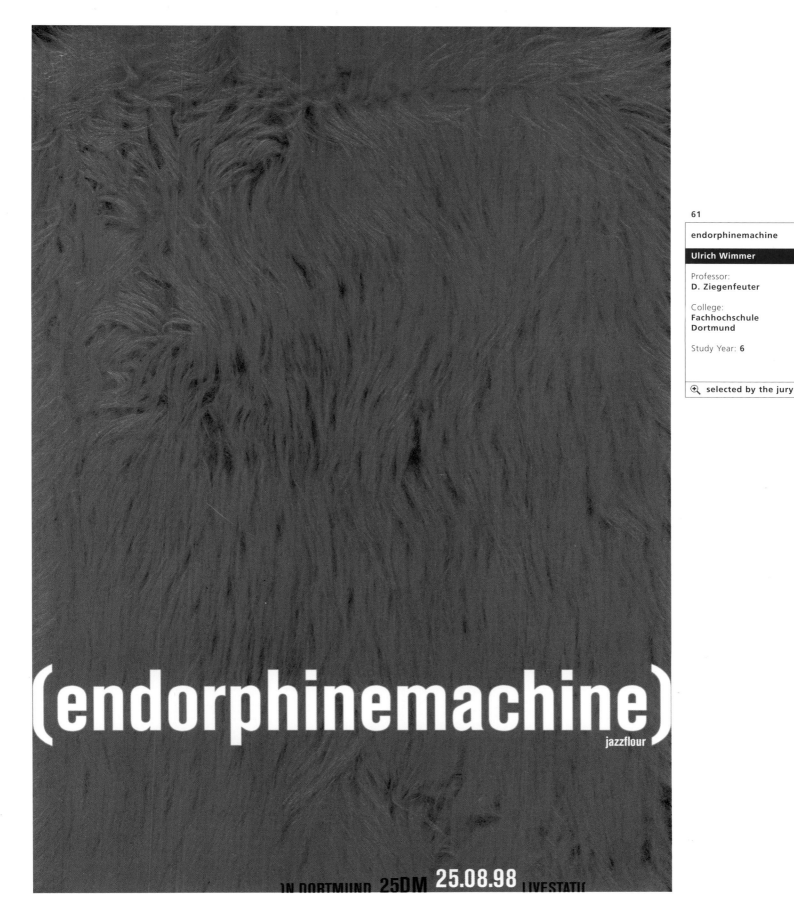

Poster for the band »endorphinemachine«. The style of this band is a mix between Dancefloor and Jazz.

Plakat für die Band »endorphinemachine«. Der Musikstil der Band ist eine Mischung aus Dancefloor und Jazz.

endorphinemachine
Ulrich Wimmer
Professor: **D. Ziegenfeuter**
College: **Fachhochschule Dortmund**
Study Year: **6**

selected by the jury

Country

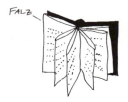

**5-days-reading
A Literature Festival
5-tage-lesen
Ein Literaturfest**

< **Gabriele Berueter**

Professor:
Polly Bertram

College:
Schule für Gestaltung Zürich

selected by the jury

↑1

Polly Bertram:

On five successive evenings, authors give readings on the themes darker, larger, better, farther and hotter (evil, urban, utopian, exotic and erotic) in the industrial quarter in Zurich in especially selected locations. The advertising materials are program flyers about the individual evenings in addition to printed plastic ribbons; a sophisticatedly designed reader will be published for the literary celebration.

The reader as a sampler who puts together any conceivable story from a set of 26 symbols is the conceptional starting point of this work. Five picture fonts were realized for the five evenings that enter into a dialog and competition with the »legible« language and comment upon it.

1 The reader is provided with a Japanese binding. If the pages are opened up, the translation of the picture font can be read on the inside.
   Der Reader ist mit einer japanischen Bindung versehen. Trennt man die Seiten auf, kann man auf den Innenseiten die Übersetzung der Bilderschrift nachlesen.
2 Font sample sheet for one of the picture fonts
   Schriftmusterblatt zu einem der Bilderfonts
3 Program flyer »darker«
   Programmblatt »dunkler«
4 Program flyer »better«
   Programmblatt »besser«
5 Program flyer »farther«
   Programmblatt »weiter«
6 Program flyer »bigger«
   Programmblatt »größer«
7 Program flyer »hotter«
   Programmblatt »heißer«

↓2

< Country

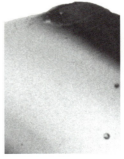

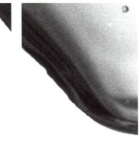

↑3 ↑4

Polly Bertram:

An fünf aufeinanderfolgenden Abenden lesen Autor/innen zu den Themenkreisen dunkler, größer, besser, weiter und heißer (Böses, Urbanes, Utopisches, Exotisches und Erotisches) im Industriequartier Zürich an eigens dazu bestimmten Örtlichkeiten. Werbemittel sind, neben bedruckten Plastikbändern mit vielfältigen Einsatzmöglichkeiten, Programmblätter zu den einzelnen Abenden; anläßlich des Literaturfestes erscheint ein aufwendig gestalteter Reader.

Der Leser als Sampler, der sich jede denkbare Geschichte aus einem Set von 26 Zeichen zusammensetzt, ist der konzeptionelle Ausgangspunkt der Arbeit. Zu den fünf Abenden wurden fünf Bilderfonts realisiert, die mit der »lesbaren« Sprache in Dialog und Konkurrenz treten und diese kommentieren.

↑5 ↓6 ↓7

**CD-Package
»Andes«**
CD-Verpackung
»Andes«

< **Svetlana Katargina**

Professor:
Boris Trofimov

College:
High Academy School of Graphic Design Moscow

Study Year: **4**

🔍 selected by the jury

Svetlana Katargina:

The design and packaging for a CD was to be created. The name, theme, representation, photography, etc. were to be developed and then realized in a model.

The »Andes« CD contains 23 well-known pieces of South American folklore music.

I chose unusual materials for the design that reflect the contemplative, mystical and enigmatic mood of the music. The cover consists of a »discus« that has the surface of a weathered stone. The CD is partially visible and glitters like a treasure through the packaging.

Aufgabe war es, eine Ausstattung zu für eine CD zu entwerfen. Dabei sollten Name, Thema, Darstellung, Fotografie usw. selber entwickelt und anschließend ein Modell angefertigt werden.

Die CD »Andes« enthält 23 bekannte Stücke südamerikanischer Folklore-Musik.

Ich habe für die Ausstattung der CD ungewöhnliche Materialien ausgewählt, die die nachdenkliche, mystische und rätselhafte Stimmung der Musik wiedergeben. Die Schutzhülle besteht aus einem »Diskus«, der die Oberfläche eines zerfressenen Steins hat. Die CD ist zum Teil sichtbar und funkelt – wie ein Schatz – aus der Packung hervor.

< Country

65

CD Package for the
music group »Kolibri«
CD-Verpackung für die
Musikgruppe »Kolibri«

Alexandra Ostrovskaja >

Professor:
Boris Trofimov

College:
**High Academy School of
Graphic Design, Moscow**

Study Year: **4**

🔍 selected by the jury

CD-Packaging for the CD
»Find 10 Differences«
of the band »Kolobri«
**The Packaging consists of
different, used materials. It is
possible – next to its function
as a protection for the CD –
to use the cover also as a wall
decoration. The images on
the front cover can be changed.**

Alexandra Ostrovskaja:

**Die Verpackung besteht aus
verschiedenen, gebrauchten
Verpackungsmaterialen. Neben
der Nutzung als Schutzhülle für
die darin befindliche CD, kann
man das Cover auch einfach
als Wandschmuck an die Wand
hängen. Dabei können die
Abbildungen je nach Lust und
Laune ausgetauscht werden.**

Country >

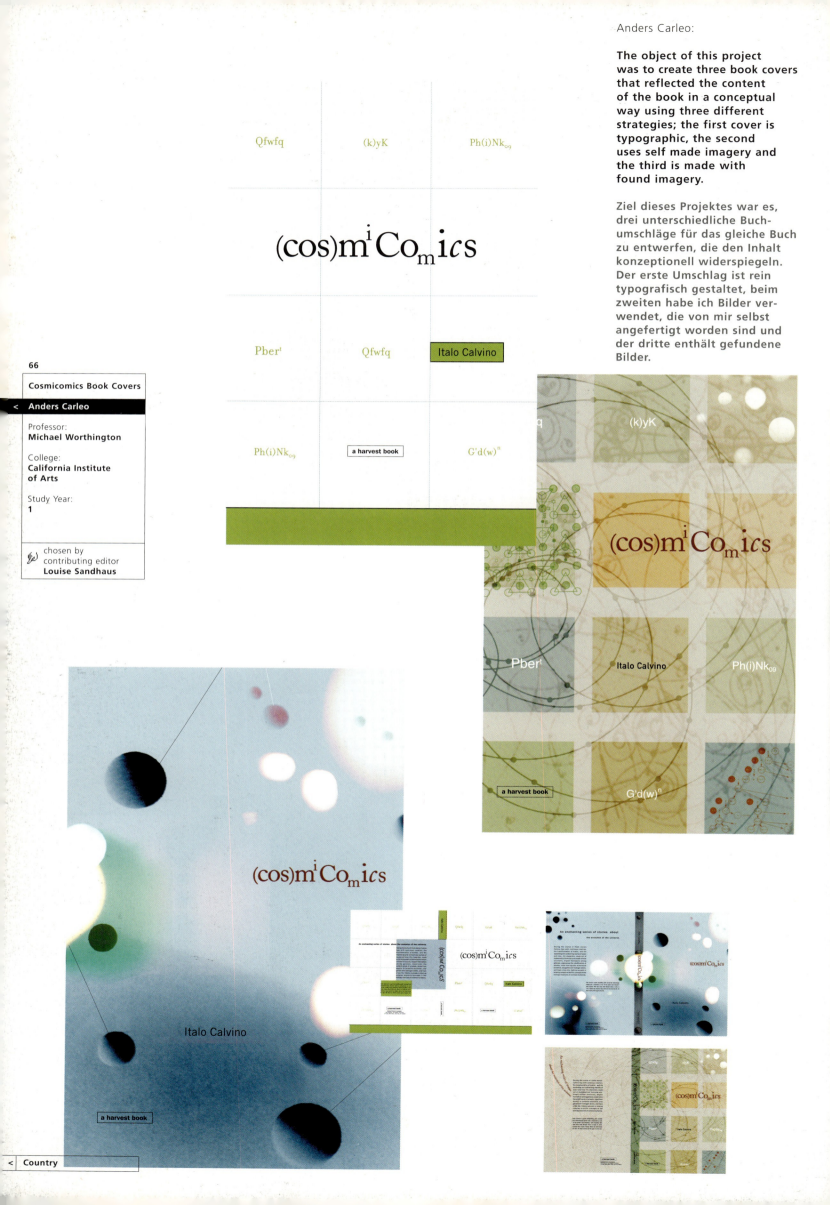

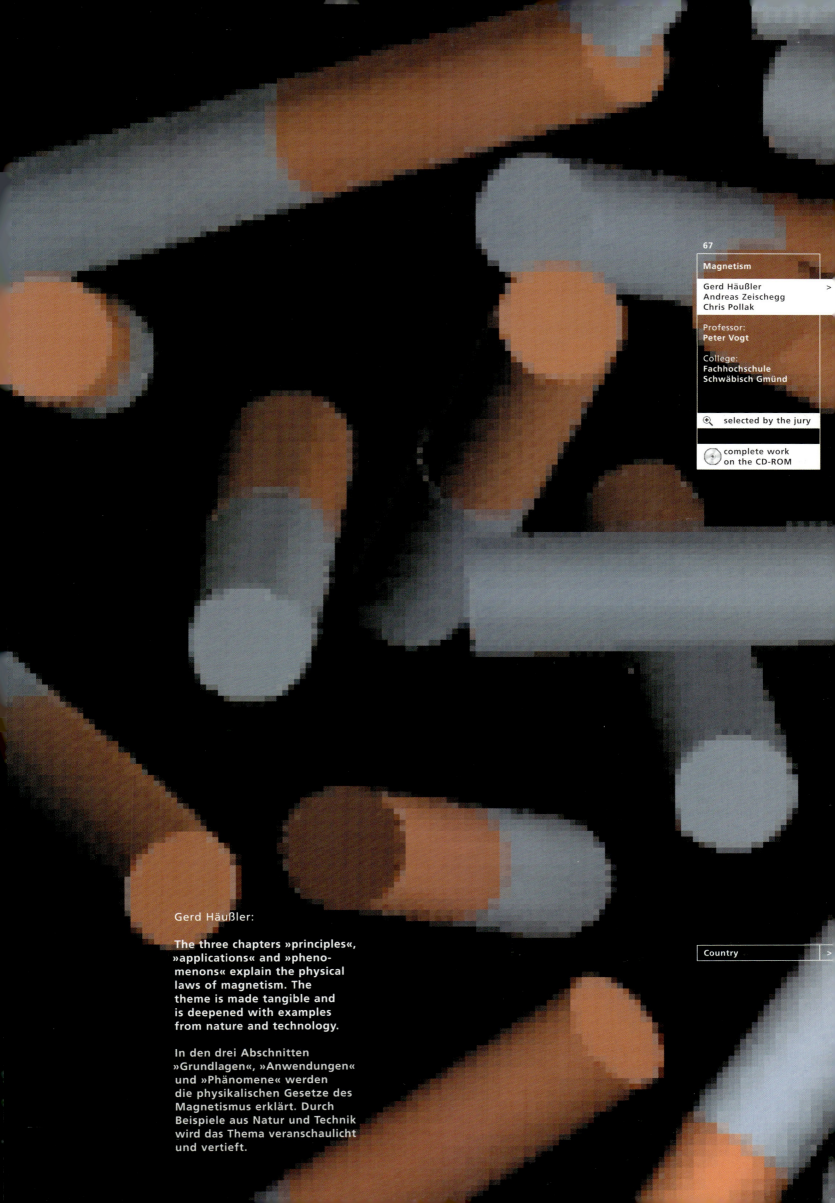

Magnetism

Gerd Häußler
Andreas Zeischegg
Chris Pollak

Professor:
Peter Vogt

College:
Fachhochschule
Schwäbisch Gmünd

selected by the jury

complete work on the CD-ROM

Gerd Häußler:

The three chapters »principles«, »applications« and »phenomenons« explain the physical laws of magnetism. The theme is made tangible and is deepened with examples from nature and technology.

In den drei Abschnitten »Grundlagen«, »Anwendungen« und »Phänomene« werden die physikalischen Gesetze des Magnetismus erklärt. Durch Beispiele aus Natur und Technik wird das Thema veranschaulicht und vertieft.

Country

The »washable name pillar« is an advertising pillar as a memorial to the Jewish as well as other victims of Nazis in Berlin.

The 55.696 names of the deported and murdered Jews from Berlin cover the entire surface (in alphabetical order) of the pillar. They are printed with water-soluble red paint so that the letters wash out from the weather and, over the course of time, run down the surface. The slow disappearance of the names symbolizes the process of forgetting and suppressing and the act of »washing away« guilt and responsibility.

In the spring of 1998, the »washable name pillar« was displayed in Koppenplatz in the former Scheunenviertel of Berlin Mitte.

Die »abwaschbare Namenssäule« ist eine Litfaßsäule, die an die jüdischen und anderen Opfer des Nationalsozialismus in Berlin erinnert.

Die 55.696 Namen der deportierten und ermordeten Juden Berlins sind flächendeckend (in alphabetischer Reihenfolge) auf die Säule gebracht. Sie sind mit wasserlöslicher roter Farbe gedruckt, so daß durch Witterungseinflüsse die Buchstaben verwaschen und im Laufe der Zeit an der Fläche herunterlaufen. Das langsame Verschwinden der Namen symbolisiert den Prozeß des Vergessens und Verdrängens der Vergangenheit und das »Reinwaschen« von Schuld und Verantwortung.

Im Frühjahr 1998 war die »abwaschbare Namenssäule« auf dem Koppenplatz im ehemaligen Scheunenviertel in Berlin Mitte zu sehen.

68 | 69

washable name pillar
abwaschbare Namenssäule

So-Hyon Choe + Sebastian Lemm + Nina Murray

Professor: **Holger Matthies**

College: **Hochschule der Künste Berlin**

Study Year: **6**

selected by the jury

Country >

Irma Schick:

I am fascinated by the strong colors, the kitsch and the many type fonts found in Indian advertising. I was surprised to see that most of the outdoor advertising is still painted by hand.

The four picture books show various areas of advertising and communication:

1 Sign book
Advertising signs on the streets of Achmedabad, Bombay and Bangalore

2 Deity book
Representation of gods on postcards and posters

3 Cinema book
Stars from the Indian movies

4 Product catalog
Products and packaging

 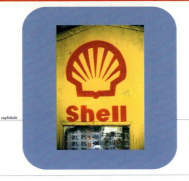

70 | 71

Book about Indian Advertising
Buch über Indische Werbung

Irma Schick

Professor:
Ulrich Namislow

College:
Fachhochschule Mainz

Study Year: 5

selected by the jury

Irma Schick:

Ich bin fasziniert von den kräftigen Farben, dem Kitsch und den vielen Schriften in der indischen Werbung. Es war neu, zu sehen, daß die Mehrzahl der Außenwerbung noch handgemalt ist. Die vier Bildbände zeigen verschiedene Bereiche von Werbung und Kommunikation:

Country >

1 Schilderbuch
Werbeschilder auf den Straßen von Achmedabad, Bombay und Bangalore

2 Götterbuch
Götterdarstellungen auf Postkarten und Plakaten

3 Kinobuch
Stars aus dem indischen Kino

4 Produktkatalog
Produkte und Verpackungen

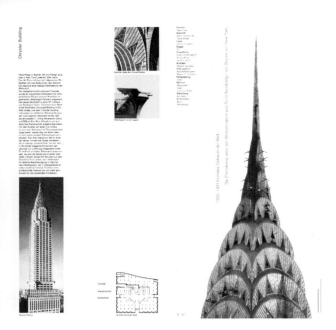

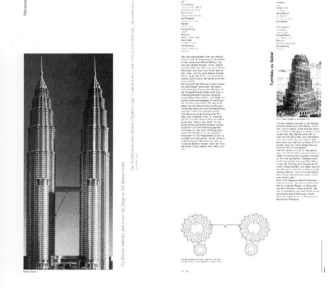

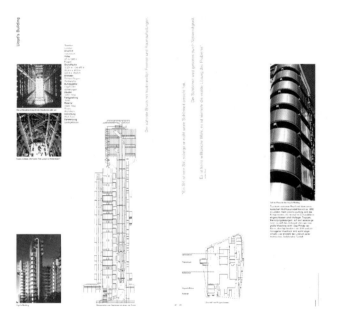

Kathrin Wackersreuther
Trudi Zwick:

Not long after man started to build, the desire to build ever-higher structures evolved. Until the 19th century, building upward toward the heaven was reserved for sacred buildings. In the time that followed, this dogma was abandoned, mainly because of the increased economic power and urbanization in the United States. New vertical landscapes were created there. The term skyscraper was the only name that could do justice to these buildings. That skyscrapers are fascinating goes without saying. For some, the reaction is positive, for others, it is negative, for some, skyscrapers represent a visionary glance into the future, for others, the embodiment of inhumanity.

The goal of the work is not to deal with the plethora of high-rise buildings but rather to offer a representative, visual overview of this niche in architecture. We chose one building for every style so that the resulting chronology takes us from the earliest beginnings to the future.

Mirror images, juxtaposition with buildings from the pre-industrial age, aimed at revealing architectural examples and common stylistic grounds.

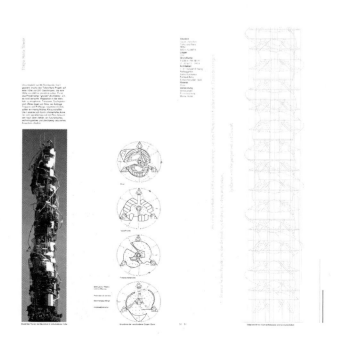

Kathrin Wackersreuther
Trudi Zwick:

Nicht lange nachdem der Mensch zu bauen begann, entstand das Streben nach Höhe. Bis ins 19. Jahrhundert war der Bau in die Höhe jedoch nur sakralen Bauten vorbehalten. In der folgenden Zeit fiel dieses Dogma; vor allen Dingen aufgrund der gestiegenen Wirtschaftskraft und der Urbanisierung in den USA. Dort entstanden neue, vertikale Landschaften. Der Begriff Wolkenkratzer war der einzige Name, der diesen Bauten gerecht werden konnte. Die Faszination der Wolkenkratzer – auch Cloudpiercer genannt – steht außer Frage. Für manche positiv, für andere negativ, für die einen als visionärer Blick in die Zukunft, für die anderen als Verkörperung der Inhumanität.

Unsere Arbeit ist eine repräsentative, visuelle Übersicht über diese Nische der Architektur. Wir haben für jede Stilrichtung ein Gebäude ausgewählt, so daß sich eine Chronologie von den Anfängen bis in die Zukunft ergibt.

Eine spiegelbildliche Gegenüberstellung mit Bauten des vorindustriellen Zeitalters soll architektonische Vorbilder und stilistische Gemeinsamkeiten aufzeigen.

Vertical Landscapes
Vertikale Landschaften

Trudi Zwick
Kathrin Wackersreuther

Professor:
Michael Burke
Jürgen Hoffmann

College:
Fachhochschule Schwäbisch Gmünd

Study Year: **4**

selected by the jury

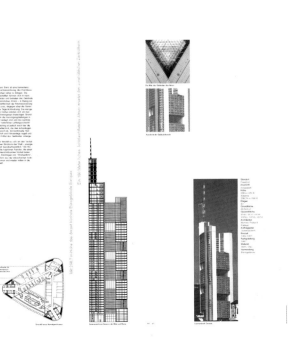
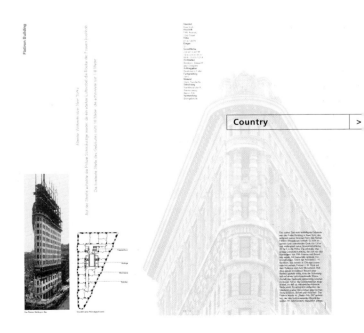

Country

Jürgen Bertram:

My approach was to photograph children in a rather unusual way. I didn't want to immortalize them in the usual way but to emphasize their independence and responsibility.

Es war mein Anspruch, Kinder in einer eher ungewöhnlichen Weise zu fotografieren. Ich wollte sie nicht im gewohnten Kindchenschema festhalten, sondern Ihre Selbständigkeit und Eigenverantwortlichkeit betonen.

74

Portrait Series Z

< Jürgen Bertram

Professor:
Inge Osswald

College:
Universität Gesamthochschule Essen

Study Year: 6

🔍 selected by the jury

< Country

Carola Thölke:

What characterizes the British? How do the Spanish differ from the French? Of what sort are the Italians? Rarely does anything one can usually think of exceed the insight of the stereotype. The image we have of others is largely determined by clichés, and nobody can seriously claim to be completely free of prejudices. Clichés are, however, similar to details: both distort perception.

Carola Thölke:

Was zeichnet die Briten aus? Worin unterscheiden sich Spanier und Franzosen? Von welchem Schlage sind die Italiener? Alles, was einem dazu einfällt kommt meist über den Erkenntnisstand eines Vorurteils nicht hinaus. Das Bild des anderen wird zu einem großen Teil von Kischees bestimmt und kein Mensch kann ernsthaft behaupten, er sei völlig frei von vorgefassten Meinungen. Klischees sind aber etwas ähnliches wie Detailaufnahmen: beide verzerren die Wahrnehmung.

75

Images of Germany
Deutschlandbilder

Carola Thölke >

Professor:
J. Graf

College:
Fachhochschule Dortmund

Study Year: 4

selected by the jury

Country >

76

Coca Cola

Ta-Li Shieh

College:
Visual Communication
Design Shih-Chien
University

selected by the jury

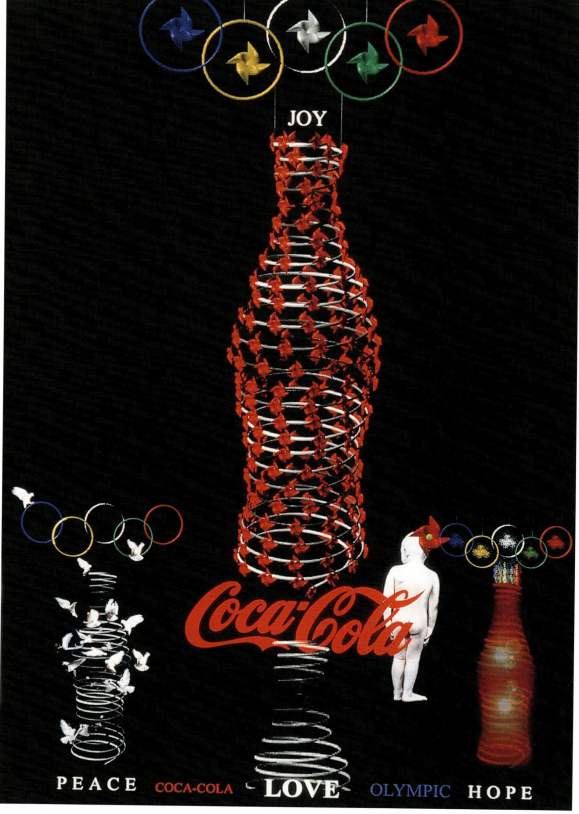

Coca-Cola

This poster has been designed to celebrate the Olympic Games 1996 in Atlanta. Chinese windmills form the shape of the coke bottle by circling it from top to the bottom.

Country

Coca-Cola

Dieses Poster wurde zur Feier der Olympischen Spiele 1996 in Atlanta entworfen. Chinesische Windmühlen bilden die Form der Coca-Cola Flasche, indem sie diese von oben nach unten umkreisen.

1998 1,79 DM

A national poster campaign on the theme »50 years of DM« was the occasion for this poster series and these postcards.

The series deals with the changing value of the German Mark by showing a selection of products that existed 50 years ago and still exist today. Confronting the D-Mark and its history, the history of this Republic, from the currency reform in 1948 to the economic miracle during the fifties and the introduction of the Euro, gave us the idea to describe the omnipresence of the D-Mark with products of every-day life and, thus, to show its loss in value in a simple, tangible and easily discernable way.

Ein bundesweiter Plakataufruf zum Thema »50 Jahre DM« war Anlaß für diese Plakatserie und Postkarten.

Die Serie beschäftigt sich mit dem Wertwandel der Deutschen Mark anhand einer Auswahl von Produkten, die es vor 50 Jahren schon gab und heute noch gibt. Die Auseinandersetzung mit der D-Mark und ihrer Geschichte – die Geschichte dieser Republik, von der Währungsreform 1948 über das Wirtschaftswunder der 50er Jahre bis hin zur Einführung des Euro – brachte uns auf die Idee, die Allgegenwärtigkeit der Deutschen Mark durch Produkte des täglichen Lebens zu schildern und somit auf schlichte und leicht zu erfassende Weise ihren Wertverlust aufzuzeigen.

0,60 DM

1998 1,69 DM

1998

77
50 Years DM
50 Jahre DM

Sandra Dörfler +
Constanze Greve >

Professor:
Gunter Rambow

College:
Hochschule für
Gestaltung Karlsruhe

Study Year: 5

🔍 selected by the jury

50 Jahre DM

Deutsche Währungsreform am 20. Juni 1948
Dokumentation der Mark – gestern und heute

0,38 DM

1998

0,05 DM

0,10 DM

1998 0,30 DM

1998

0,04 DM

50 Ja
Deutsche Währu
Dokumentation

Country >

0,05 DM

1948 0,08 DM

1948

Sonja Kampczyk:
»Speak, so I can see you« –
a campaign for »Radio 5«

At the occasion of the WDR reform in 1994, which had the goal of giving each of its five programs a more distinct profile, WDR 5 was renamed »Radio 5«. The station was to become a talk radio station following the example of »Radio Four« of BBC: a pure spoken program with sophisticated journalism and radiophonic art. Its framework was formed by information programs. Reports, documentaries, talks, advisories, radio plays and programs for children as well as educational programs complete the offering. In the evening, the program is rounded off with foreign-language programs and special music programs.

The work concentrates on showing the context between the radio broadcast and the human reception. The selection of the subjects points at the way the sound waves travel through the ether to the recipient: they float through the air, find the private world of the human, pass through house walls and reach the individual where he or she lives and feels at home. »Radio 5 permeates«. Living room becomes listening room.

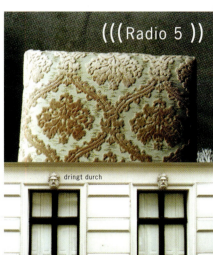

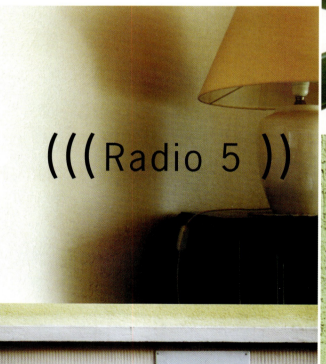

dringt durch

(((Radio 5)))

Sonja Kampczyk:

»Sprich, damit ich Dich sehe«
eine Kampagne für »Radio 5«
Im Zuge der Reform des WDR von 1994, bei der angestrebt wurde, seine fünf Programme klarer zu profilieren, wurde WDR 5 umbenannt in »Radio 5«. Der Sender sollte zu einer Wortwelle nach dem Vorbild von »Radio Four« des BBC werden: ein reines Wortprogramm mit anspruchsvollem Journalismus und radiophoner Kunst. Sein eigentliches Gerüst bilden Informationssendungen. Reportagen, Dokumentationen, Gespräche, Ratgeber, Hörspiele sowie Kindersendungen und Bildungsprogramme ergänzen das Angebot. Am Abend wird das Programm durch Fremdsprachensendungen und spezielle Musiksendungen abgerundet.

Die Arbeit konzentriert sich darauf, den Zusammenhang »Radio sendet« und »Mensch empfängt« darzustellen. Die Auswahl der Sujets deutet den Weg an, den die Schallwellen durch den Äther zum Empfänger zurücklegen: Sie schweben durch die Luft, finden die private Welt des Menschen, gehen durch Häuserwände und erreichen den Einzelnen da, wo er lebt und sich zu Hause fühlt. »Radio 5 dringt durch«. Wohnraum wird zum Hör-Raum.

Radio 5	
Sonja Kampczyk	>
Professor: Uwe Loesch	
College: Gesamthochschule Wuppertal	
selected by the jury	

| Country | > |

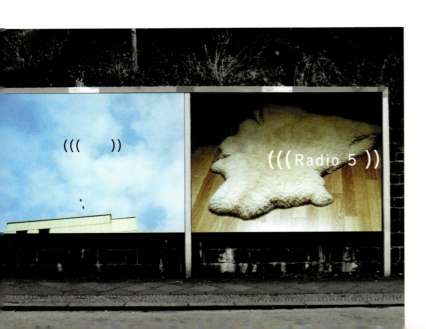

›klarheit‹

Unaufhörlich wächst die Informations- und Bilderflut unserer Zeit und überfordert unsere Wahrnehmung. Um der visuellen Überreizung zu entkommen, sucht unser Auge nach Klarheit.

Moderne Messe- und Architektursysteme bedürfen einer klaren Aussage – reduziert auf die Präsenz purer Ästhetik. Damit die Botschaft eines Unternehmens und seiner Produkte klar kommuniziert wird. Klarheit aber auch in der Funktion – selbsterklärende Verbindungsprinzipien, die die Montage systematisch erleichtern. Denn das Einfache hat System.

Gern senden wir Ihnen weitere Informationen oder nennen Ihnen einen unserer Partner weltweit.

Burkhardt Leitner constructiv
Messe- und Ausstellungssysteme
Am Bismarckturm 39
D-70192 Stuttgart
Telefon +49 711.2 55 88-0
Telefax +49 711.2 55 88-11
E-mail info@burkhardtleitner.de
www.burkhardtleitner.de

BURKHARDT LEITNER constructiv

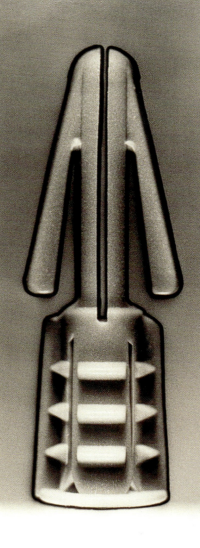

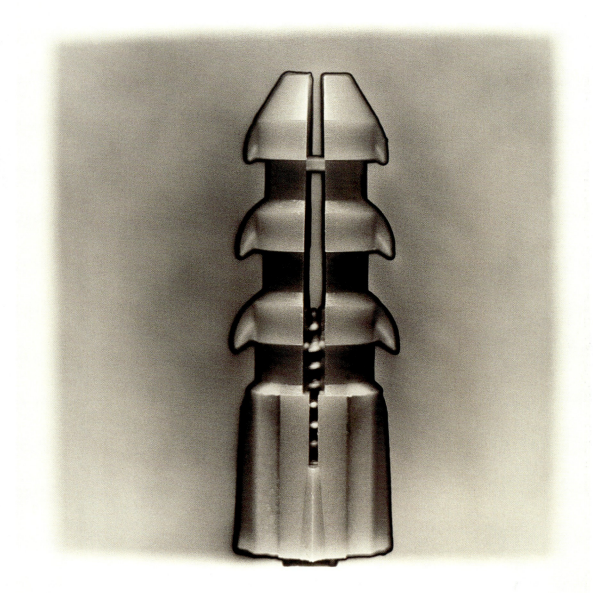

Photography and Darkroom Process
Fotografie und Dunkelkammerprozeß

Andrew Ecclestone

Professor:
**Neil Grant
Stephen Raw**

College:
Manchester Metropolitain University

chosen by contributing editor
Neil Grant

Photography experimenting on the transformation of the mundane through the medium of photography and darkroom processes. Both images are of industrial wall fixings given an iconic quality through the action of photographer and medium.

Fotografie, die mit der Transformation des eEinfachen durch die Medien Fotografie und Dunkelkammerprozesse experimentiert. Beide Bilder zeigen Wanddübel und erhalten durch den Eingriff des Fotografen und die Nutzung des Mediums eine ikonische Qualität.

Country >

Exhibition on occasion of the Day of Water
Ausstellung zum Tag des Wassers

Katja Gretzinger

Professors:
Prof. Hagenberg
Prof. Meussen

College:
Fachhochschule Düsseldorf

Study Year: 6

selected by the jury

Country

Katja Gretzinger:

The focal theme of my work is the perception of water in modern society. In our technological world, water is often reduced to formulas, its substrates and derivatives. Symbolic and philosophical aspects of water, however, seem to have been lost in our society. A book and a public space exhibition were created for this purpose.

The book is organized in an image level that is accompanied by two different levels of story telling. One level follows scientific positions from chemistry and physics to geology and history. The second level shows a rather subjective, emotional and spiritual-historic approach to water. It contains quotes and text passages of various authors from the fields of philosophy, poetry and fiction.

In line with the essence of water, a cycle evolves at the end of which the observer finds himself back at the beginning: the vision of the genesis of new life beyond the earth that is connected with the existence of water according to science.

The »Day of the Water« is the impulse for an exhibition that takes place throughout the entire city. People are not invited to a specific event. Rather, the usual environment is changed by markings or signs pointing at »water sites«.

For example, chalk »stamps« signalize the presence of water, stamps that will eventually be dissolved by water.

Our stereotypical image of blue water is an incomplete perception. Moreover, water is a medium for all life-essential substances. It takes on their colors, red in our blood, green like the algae of a pond or brown and orange in colored drinks.

Katja Gretzinger:

Schwerpunkt meiner Arbeit ist die Wahrnehmung des Wassers in der modernen Gesellschaft. In unserer technisierten Welt wird Wasser vielfach auf Formeln, seine Substrate und Derivate reduziert. Symbolische und philosophische Aspekte des Wassers hingegen scheinen unserer Gesellschaft verlorengegangen zu sein. Hierzu entstanden ein Buch und eine Ausstellung im öffentlichen Raum.

Das Buch gliedert sich in eine Bildebene, die von zwei unterschiedlichen Erzählebenen begleitet wird. Die eine Ebene verfolgt wissenschaftliche Positionen von der Chemie über die Physik und die Geologie bis hin zur Geschichtsschreibung. Die zweite Ebene zeigt eine eher subjektive, emotionale und geistesgeschichtliche Auseinandersetzung mit Wasser. Sie beinhaltet Zitate und Textpassagen verschiedener Autorinnen und Autoren aus den Gebieten der Philosophie, der Poesie und der Belletristik.

Dem Wesen des Wassers entsprechend, ergibt sich so ein Kreislauf, an dessen Ende sich der Betrachter wieder am Anfang sieht: bei der Vision von der Entstehung neuen Lebens außerhalb der Erde, die sich nach Meinung der Wissenschaft an die Existenz von Wasser knüpft.

Der »Tag des Wassers« ist Anlass für eine Ausstellung im ganzen Stadtraum. Die Menschen werden nicht gezielt zu einer Veranstaltung gebeten. Vielmehr wird die gewohnte Umgebung verändert – durch Auszeichnungen oder Kennzeichnungen von »Wasser-Orten«. So signalisieren z.B. »Stempelungen« mit Kreide das Vorhandensein von Wasser, Stempelungen, die selber wieder durch Wasser aufgelöst werden.

Unser stereotypes Bild des blauen Wassers ist eine unvollständige Wahrnehmung. Vielmehr ist Wasser Medium für alle lebenswichtigen Stoffe. Es nimmt deren Farben an, rot in unserem Blut, grün wie die Algen eines Teichs oder braun oder orange in gefärbten Getränken.

→ *Stamps at water-locations*
   Stempelung an Wasser-Orten

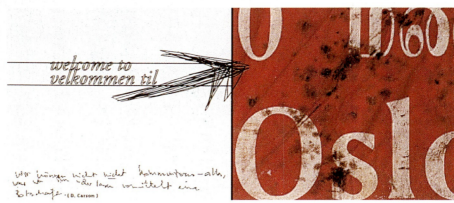

Book about Eastern Oslo
Buch über Ost-Oslo

< **Irina Futivic**

Professor:
Josef Leupi

College:
Faculdade de Belas Artes de Lisboa

Study Year: **5**

🔍 selected by the jury

Irina Futivic:

Oslo is divided by a river into two parts, the »Vestkanten« and the »Østkanten«, which is situated east of the river Aker. »Østkanten« is generally inhabited by people of a worse economic situation; especially by a lot of foreigners from Asia and Africa.

After a 2 minutes walk from downtown you seem to enter a different world, where life is lived in a different, and in comparison with the wealthy and very organised western Oslo, very chaotic way. It has its own visual language and aesthetics.

I was shocked and amazed at the same time about this part of the town. The book can be seen as a journey through the area trying to »translate« these impressions in a two-dimensional manner.

Irina Futivic:

Oslo wird von einem Fluß in zwei Teile geteilt, die »Vestkanten« und die »Østkanten«, die sich östlich des Flusses Aker befinden.

»Østkanten« ist eine Gegend, in der generell Menschen leben, denen es wirtschaftlich nicht sehr gut geht; vor allem viele Ausländer aus Asien und Afrika.

Nach 2 Minuten Fußweg vom Stadtzentrum scheint man eine andere Welt zu betreten, in der das Leben anders und – verglichen mit dem sehr organisierten westlichen Oslo – sehr chaotisch abläuft. Es besitzt eine eigene Bildsprache und Ästhetik.

Ich war von diesem Stadtteil zugleich schockiert und erstaunt. Das Buch kann als eine Reise durch die Gegend verstanden werden, die diese Impressionen zweidimensional zu übersetzen versucht.

< Country

Genius is 1% inspiration and 99% perspiration. But genius and $2.25 will get you a double-decaf Mochaccino. The extra 2% you need to get your genuis between buckram covers or into a bubble-back with foil-stamping and onto a shelf at the mall is passion. Though in-class and studio assignments students will explore their personal passions and use them as the bases for real and imaginary projects.

Assignment: Find a free object and package it in order to make it valuable.

Genie ist 1% Inspiration und 99% Schweiß. Doch Genie und $2.25 bringen einem einen doppelten, koffeinfreien Mochaccino. Die extra 2%, die man braucht, um sein Genie zwischen Buckram-Einbände oder in eine Blister-folie mit Prägung und dann auf ein Regal im Einkaufszentrum zu bringen, bestehen aus Leidenschaft. Die Studenten erfahren durch die Aufgaben ihre persönlichen Leiden-schaften und setzen diese als Basis für reale und imaginäre Projekte ein.

Aufgabe: finde ein beliebiges Objekt und verpacke es, um es wertvoll zu machen.

87

Chelsea to go

Amy Unikewicz

Professor:
Steven Guarnaccia

College:
School of Visual Arts
New York

chosen by contributing editor
Steven Heller

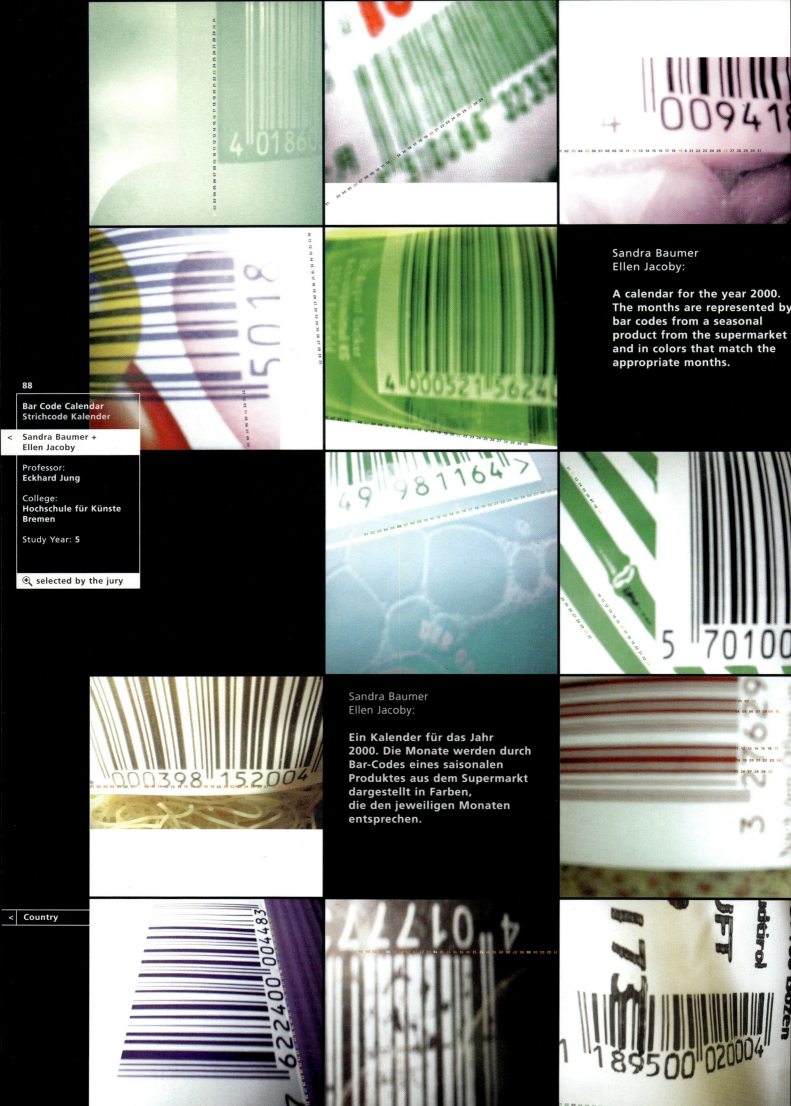

Bar Code Calendar
Strichcode Kalender

< Sandra Baumer +
Ellen Jacoby

Professor:
Eckhard Jung

College:
Hochschule für Künste
Bremen

Study Year: 5

selected by the jury

Sandra Baumer
Ellen Jacoby:

A calendar for the year 2000.
The months are represented by
bar codes from a seasonal
product from the supermarket
and in colors that match the
appropriate months.

Sandra Baumer
Ellen Jacoby:

Ein Kalender für das Jahr
2000. Die Monate werden durch
Bar-Codes eines saisonalen
Produktes aus dem Supermarkt
dargestellt in Farben,
die den jeweiligen Monaten
entsprechen.

< Country

Poster to announce a lecture about »Newspapers and Magazines in the Era of electronic networks« at the College of Design Karlsruhe, Germany.

Newspapers and Magazines in the Era of Electronic Networks
Zeitungen und Magazine im Zeitalter elektronischer Vernetzung

Constanze Greve

Professor:
Gunter Rambow

College:
Hochschule für Gestaltung Karlsruhe

selected by the jury

Country

Paris

- □ Cafés
- • Museums
- ■ Archtecture and Landmark
- ◆ Colleges
- ✦ Opéra and Théâtre

Designed by Charles Girault, this grand 19th-century exhibition hall is still used for major displays.

Monmartre · Musée de Montmartre ■
· Sacré-Cœur

High on its nothern hill overlooking Paris, Montmartre was long linked with the artistic community that scraped a living there.

In the 18th century this former royal palace was a setting for brilliant gatherings, debauchery and gambling. Today modern sculptures grace the square.

Palais des Congres ■   Arc de Triomphe ■   · Musée Jacquemart Andre   ✦ Opéra de Paris Garnier   Tuileries Quarter

Elegant squares, formal gardens, street arcades and courtyards give this part of Paris its special character. Monuments to monarchy and the arts coexist with contemporary luxury.

The Islands

· Musée de l'Homme
· Musée de la Marine   ■ Palais de Chaillot   ■ Palais Galliera   · La Madeleine   Jardin du Palais Royal
   Jardins du Trocadéro   Cinémathèque Française   Grand Palais · Petit Palais   Champs-Elysées ■   Palais royal
                                                                                                                         · Musée du Louvre
                                                        · Palais de l'Elysée   Jardin des Tuileries

Donkey rides are a popular attraction in these formal gardens, which were designed by the royal gradener Andé Le Nôtre in the 17th century.

Palais de la...
Home to French ki[ngs] for almost four centuries, the Louvre is now a museum with one of the wor[ld's] great art collections

Tower Eiffel   **Invalides and Eiffel Tower Quarter**   · Assemblée Nationale   · Musée d'Orsay   Institut
                                                                                                       St.-Germain
                                                                                                       Les Deux M[agots]
        ■ Hôtel des Invalides
                               By the time he died in 1917, Auguste Rodin had revolutionized the art of sculpture. All his key works, including **The Thinker** *(about 1880), are on display.*
        ■ Dôme Church   · Musée Rodin   ◆ Université
                                                                                                   Paris V
   ■ Ecole Militaire   □ □
      ■ UNESCO Headquarters   □ Café de Flore

It rose to fame when Sartre and Simone de Beauvoir set up literary shop there during World War II

90 | 91

Rivers
Flüsse

< **Chae Lee**

Professor:
Ken Hiebert

College:
The University of the Arts Philadelphia

Study Year: **4**

chosen by contributing editor
Ken Hiebert

Legendary meeting places still exist, haunted by <u>the shadows of the literary and artistic gurus of the 1920s and '30s,</u> yet its main boulevards have lost much of their charm, sacrificed to the whims of latterday consumerism.

Europe's second-tallest tower
· Tour
Momtparnasse

Montparnasse

Modern incursions are rare and the atmosphere still has something of the **Paris of history, literature,** and **cinema.** The pace seems more leisurely than on the other side of the river, cafés still play their traditional role.

< Country

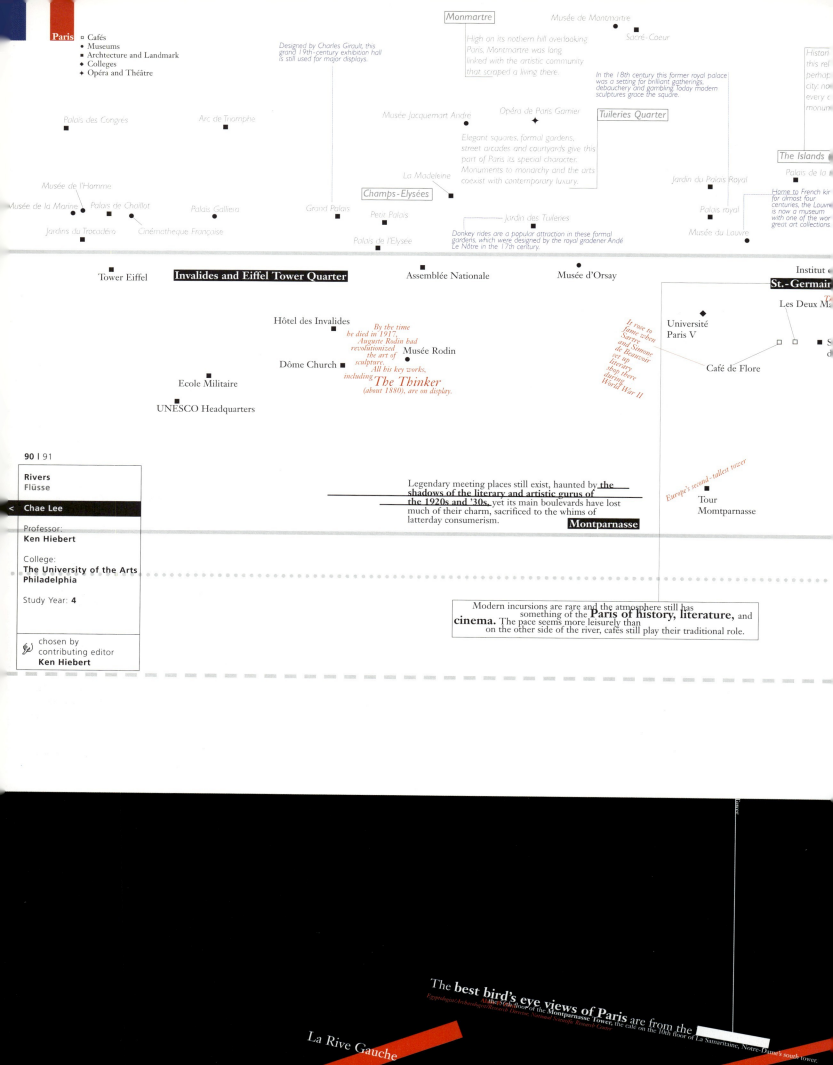

The **best bird's eye views of Paris** are from the...
La Rive Gauche
From Left Bank
To rest in the gardens of the **Musée Rodin,** taking in its beautiful sculptures.
Jardin du Luxembourg

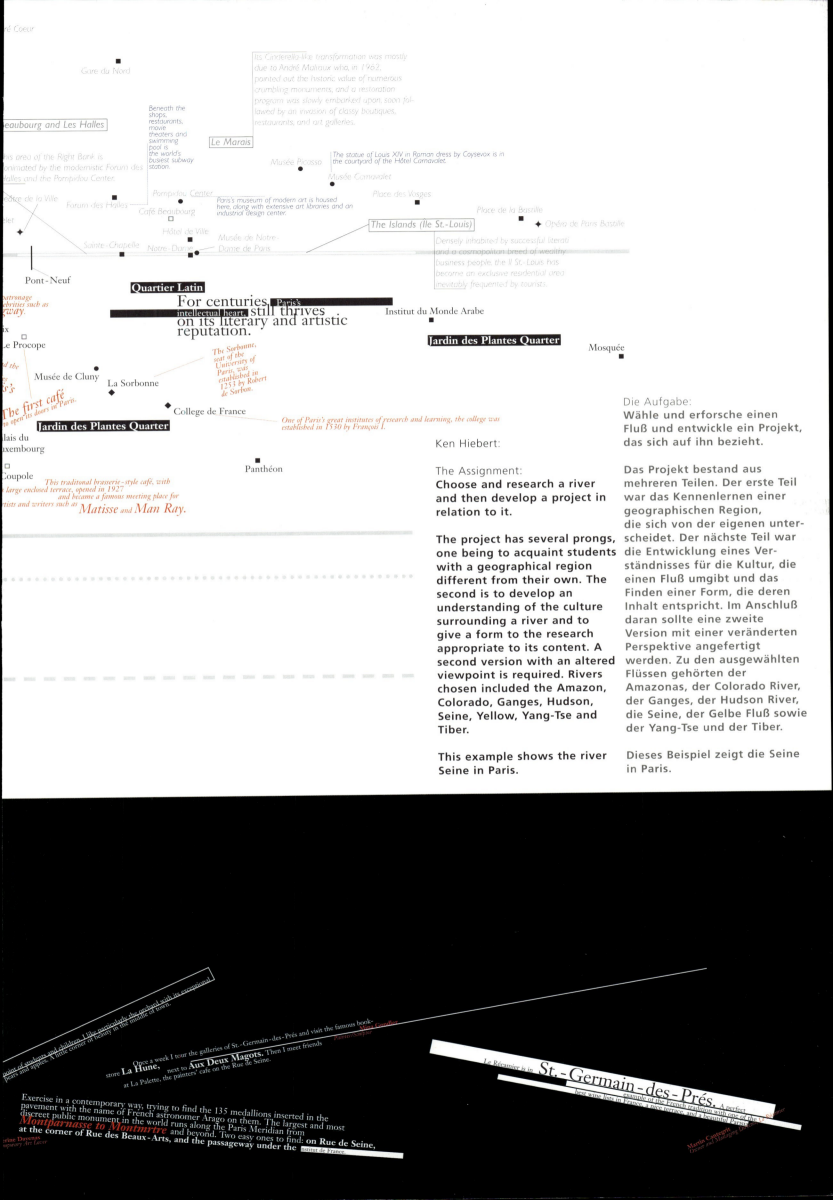

Ken Hiebert:

The Assignment:
Choose and research a river and then develop a project in relation to it.

The project has several prongs, one being to acquaint students with a geographical region different from their own. The second is to develop an understanding of the culture surrounding a river and to give a form to the research appropriate to its content. A second version with an altered viewpoint is required. Rivers chosen included the Amazon, Colorado, Ganges, Hudson, Seine, Yellow, Yang-Tse and Tiber.

This example shows the river Seine in Paris.

Die Aufgabe:
Wähle und erforsche einen Fluß und entwickle ein Projekt, das sich auf ihn bezieht.

Das Projekt bestand aus mehreren Teilen. Der erste Teil war das Kennenlernen einer geographischen Region, die sich von der eigenen unterscheidet. Der nächste Teil war die Entwicklung eines Verständnisses für die Kultur, die einen Fluß umgibt und das Finden einer Form, die deren Inhalt entspricht. Im Anschluß daran sollte eine zweite Version mit einer veränderten Perspektive angefertigt werden. Zu den ausgewählten Flüssen gehörten der Amazonas, der Colorado River, der Ganges, der Hudson River, die Seine, der Gelbe Fluß sowie der Yang-Tse und der Tiber.

Dieses Beispiel zeigt die Seine in Paris.

↑ *Weigeles dictionary*
Weigeles Lexikon

← *Free Series*
Freie Serie

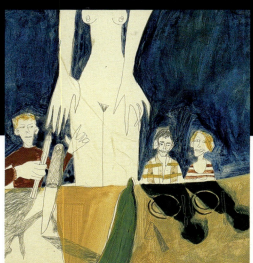

92 | 93

Illustrations

Stefanie Weigele

Professor:
Wolfgang Jarchow
Bernd Bexte

College:
Hochschule für Künste Bremen

Study Year: 6

selected by the jury

↑ *Sketch Book*
Skizzenbuch

↓ *Illustrations for DASA (German Aerospace Agency)*
Illustrationen für die DASA

Die F-Baureihe
Eine Familienchronik der Profi-Modelle von Nikon

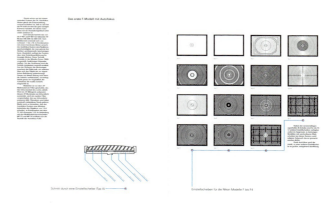

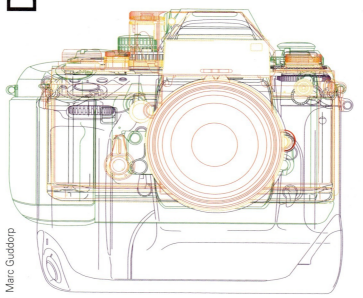

Nikon F3

Nikon F4

Nikon F5

94

The F Series
Die F-Baureihe

Marc Guddorp

Professor:
Hartmut Brückner

College:
Fachhochschule Münster

Study Year: **4**

selected by the jury

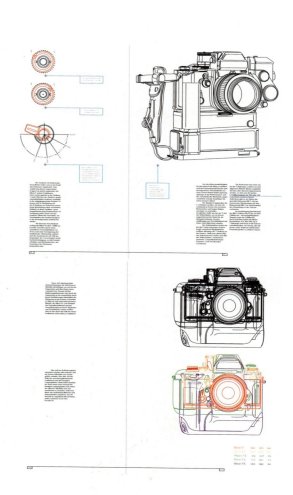

Mark Guddorp:

The book shows the development of the product line of the F-series by Nikon. Above all, ergonomics, the design and the operation of the different models is explained.

Das Buch stellt die Entwicklung der Produktfamilie der Kameras der F-Baureihe von Nikon vor. Dabei wird vor allen Dingen die Ergonomie, das Design und die Bedienung der unterschiedlichen Modelle erklärt.

Country

The changes in the product design can be compared by way of the superimposed line drawings of the five camera models on the title.

The A3 format enables the depiction of the camera on a 1:1 scale.

Anhand der sich überlagernden Strichzeichnungen der fünf Kameramodelle auf dem Titel lassen sich die Veränderungen im Produktdesign miteinander vergleichen.

Das Format A3 ermöglicht die Abbildung der Kamera im Maßstab 1:1.

95

e-mail

Christiane Gödde

Professor:
Johannes Graf

College:
Fachhochschule Dortmund

Study Year: **6**

selected by the jury

Country

Marta Josa Fresno
(Student):

This work is a prevention campaign against sexually transmitted diseases in rural communities. Starting with a fictional client, the Red Cross, and considering the high development of AIDS in South Africa, I established a graphic system adapted to the informative campaigns for the prevention of sexually transmitted diseases, STD and AIDS.
The project has three parts:

(1) A consulting library about STD and AIDS as well as life and culture in rural communities.

(2) Informative dossiers for the NGO about how they should bring the campaign forward.

(3) A graphic system realized with pictograms and aimed at rural communities with the goal of offering people an orientation about sexually transmitted diseases.

José Baltanàs
(Professor):

The project had anticipated great difficulties since it implicates the design of a pictographic system for a foreign culture. The collection of documentation has guaranteed an easy and identifiable graphic solution for the communities it is designed for. Thanks to the capacity of stylistic synthesis and the sensibility shown in the treatment of line, proportion and color, this system of signs has an impressive visual intensity without being aggressive, despite the nature of the subject.

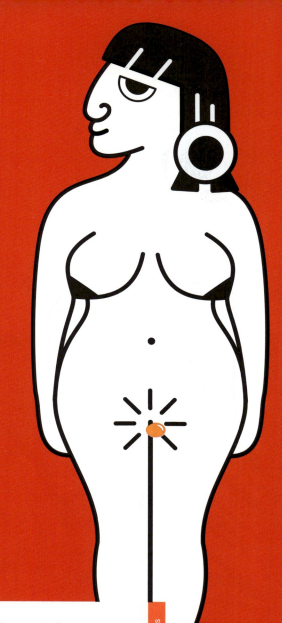

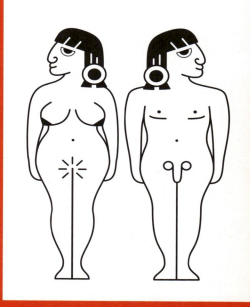

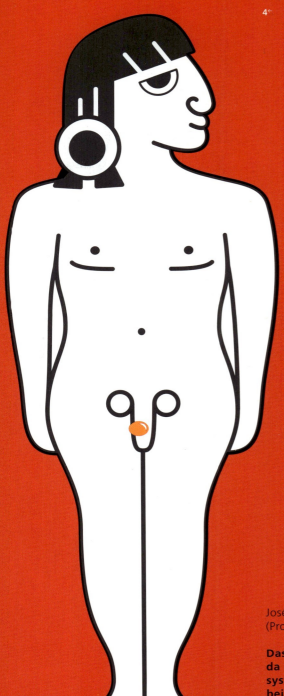

4 ←

1   The information leaflets show the different ways the infection can occur …
Auf den Informationskarten ist zu sehen, welche unterschiedlichen Infektionswege Geschlechtskrankheiten haben können…

2   …and how you can protect yourself
… und wie man sich dagegen schützen kann

3   The manual for the staff of the Red Cross describes how the didactic material should be used.
Das Handbuch für die Mitarbeiter des Roten Kreuzes beschreibt, wie das didaktische Material verwendet werden soll.

4   In the depiction of the human body, the ethnic distinctions were enhanced in order to increase identification.
Bei der Darstellung des menschlichen Körpers wurden die ethnischen Besonderheiten betont, um die Identifikation zu erhöhen.

Marta Josa Fresno (Student):

Diese Arbeit ist eine Aufklärungskampagne gegen sexuell übertragbare Krankheiten in der ländlichen Bevölkerung. Ausgehend von einem fiktiven Kunden, dem Roten Kreuz, und unter Berücksichtigung der weiten Verbreitung von AIDS in Südafrika, habe ich ein graphisches System entwickelt, das den Informationskampagnen für die Vermeidung sexuell übertragbarer Krankheiten, STD und AIDS, angepaßt ist.

Das Projekt besteht aus drei Teilen:

(1) Eine beratende Bibliothek über STD und AIDS sowie das Leben und die Kultur in der ländlichen Bevölkerung.

(2) Informationsdossiers für die NGO mit Anregungen, wie die Kampagne verbreitet werden kann.

(3) Ein graphisches System, das mit Piktogrammen umgesetzt wurde und sich an die ländliche Bevölkerung richtet, mit dem Ziel, die Menschen über sexuell übertragbare Krankheiten zu informieren.

José Baltanàs (Professor):

Das Projekt war nicht einfach, da es das Design eines Zeichensystems für eine fremde Kultur beinhaltet. Die Sammlung von Dokumentationsmaterial hat eine einfache und erkennbare grafische Lösung für die Zielgruppe ermöglicht, auf die es ausgerichtet ist. Dank der stilistischen Synthese und der Feinfühligkeit, die in der Behandlung von Linie, Proportion und Farbe angewandt wurden, ist dieses Zeichensystem visuell sehr intensiv ohne jedoch – trotz der Thematik – aggressiv zu sein.

96 | 97

Prevention Campaign for Native Communities
Vorsorge Kampagne für Eingeborenen-Völker

Marta Josa Fresno >

Professor:
Lluis Lannes
José Baltanas

College:
ESDI – Escola Superior de Dissny Barcelona

Study Year: 4

🔍 selected by the jury

1 ↓

 usar condón
 mantener relaciones sólo con tu pareja
 mantenerse en higiene

Country >

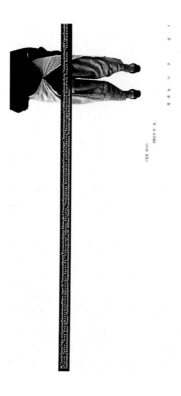

Ryu Eun:

d5 is an issue of the »d...« magazine (d1, d2, d3, etc.) published by students at the College of Fine Arts in Seoul.

The magazine tries to find different answers to the question about Korea's identity. In every issue, an outstanding cultural personality is presented and interviewed. The present issue, d5, deals with the Korean installation artist Bul Lee.

98
d5
Culture Magazin

< Ryu Eun

Professor:
Ahn Sang-Soo

College:
College of Fine Arts
Seoul

selected by the jury

Ryu Eun:

d5 ist eine Ausgabe des Magazins »d...«, (d1, d2, d3 usw.), das von Studenten am College of Fine Arts in Seoul herausgegeben wird.

Das Magazin versucht, unterschiedliche Antworten auf die Frage nach der Identität Koreas zu finden. In jeder Ausgabe wird eine andere herausragende Persönlichkeit aus dem kulturellen Bereich vorgestellt und interviewt. Die vorliegende Ausgabe d5 beschäftigt sich mit der koreanischen Installationskünstlerin Bul Lee.

< Country

99

Font: Toasted

Heike Burkhardt >

Professor:
Hans Dieter Reichert

College:
Bath College of Higher Education

Study Year: **5**

🔍 selected by the jury

Heike Burkhardt
Font »Toasted«:

»...in toasted bread I found the ideal material for my purposes. And since England is always connected in my mind with the high consumption of toast. I really think this material is appropriate for a work on British soil.«

»...Im Toastbrot fand ich ideales Material für meine Zwecke. Und da sich England für mich gedanklich immer auch mit dem dort zur genüge konsumierten Toastbrot verbindet, fand ich dieses Material wirklich angemessen für eine Arbeit auf britischem Boden.«

Country >

Jacek Mrowczyk:

Safety in the Workplace
The posters »Don't lose your head« (1) and »Computer« (2) were a contribution to a competition that the »Central Institute for Safety in the Workplace« in Warsaw holds on a regular basis. The theme of this year's competition was »Computer« in connection with the problem of »Safety in the Workplace«.

A workplace without a computer is hardly imaginable these days. But even if the speed and efficiency of the work may be increased through them, computers represent inherent hazards to health: joint pain, back and eye pain and headaches are often the consequences of computer work.

The poster »Don't lose your Head« won the 2nd prize in the competition and was awarded the special award of the 18th international graphic design biennial in Brno.

100

Don't lose your Head + Computer

< Jacek Mrowczyk

Professor:
L'ubomir Longauer

College:
Acadmy of Fine Arts and Design in Bratislava

Study Year: 4

⊕ selected by the jury

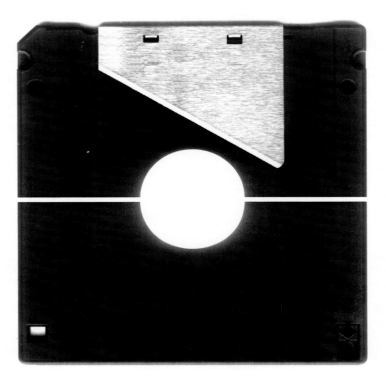

nie trać głowy

↑1 »Don't lose your head«
    »Verliere nicht den Kopf«

< Country

Jacek Mrowczyk:

Sicherheit am Arbeitsplatz
Die Plakate »Verliere nicht den Kopf« (1) und »Computer« (2) waren ein Beitrag zu einem Wettbewerb, der regelmäßig vom zentralen Institut für Arbeitssicherheit in Warschau ausgeschrieben wird. Thema des diesjährigen Wettbewerbs war »Computer« – verbunden mit der Problematik »Sicherheit am Arbeitsplatz«.

Ein Arbeitsplatz ohne Computer ist heutzutage kaum mehr vorstellbar. Doch auch wenn dadurch die Geschwindigkeit und Effizienz der Arbeit gesteigert werden, bergen Computer Gefahren für die Gesundheit: Gelenk-, Rücken-, Augen- und Kopfschmerzen sind die Folgen von Arbeit am Computer.

Das Plakat »Verliere nicht den Kopf« hat beim Wettbewerb den 2. Preis gewonnen und wurde mit dem Sonderpreis der 18. Internationalen Grafik-Design Biennale in Brno ausgezeichnet.

Tobias Klauser:

The task was to visualize the four connected terms »regional,« »national«, »international« and »global« with purely typographic means. The question as to the contexts these four terms appear in and their references to other terms, such as share of the population and economic organizations, stood in the foreground.

On the top part of the folder there is a diary entry of a killer on the run. On the left side the population numbers are noted with the appropriate terms, and a table on the right side lists the economic organizations.

Aufgabe war es, die vier zusammengehörenden Begriffe »regional«, »national«, »international« und »global« mit rein typografischen Mitteln zu visualisieren. Die Frage, in welchem Zusammenhang diese vier Begriffe auftauchen und ihre Bezüge zu anderen Begriffen wie Bevölkerungsanteil und Wirtschaftsorganisationen stand dabei im Vordergrund.

Auf dem oberen Teil des Faltbogens ist jeweils ein Tagebucheintrag eines Mörders festgehalten, der sich auf der Flucht befindet. Auf der linken Seite sind die Bevölkerungszahlen zu den betreffenden Begriffen vermerkt und in einer Tabelle auf der rechten Seite werden die entsprechenden wirtschaftlichen Organisationen genannt.

102

From regional to global
Von regional zu global

< **Tobias Klauser**

Professor:
Hans-Peter Dubacher

College:
Schule für Gestaltung Luzern

Study Year: **4**

selected by the jury

< Country

Poster for the »smart« car
Plakat für den Smart

Esther Mildenberger:

The exhibition guide and catalogue documents projects of the graduates from the department »architecture and interior design« at the Royal College of Art in London. The structure and layout of the book reflect the structure of the department: the three parallel courses are marked by orange, blue and green.

The presented work deals with the sensory space between reality and virtuality.

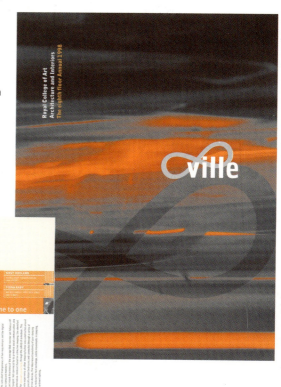

ville

< **Esther Mildenberger**

College:
Royal College of Arts

Study Year: **4**

chosen by contributing editor
Florian Pfeffer

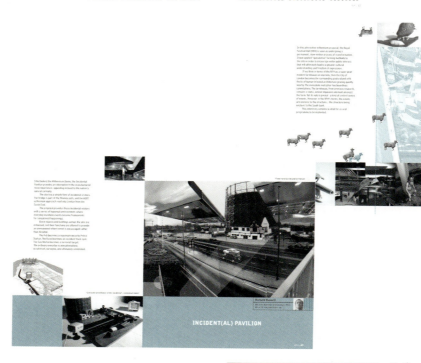

< Country

Esther Mildenberger:

Der Ausstellungsführer und Katalog dokumentiert die Abschlußarbeiten des Studienbereichs »Architektur und Innenarchitektur« am Royal College of Art in London. Aufbau und Layout des Buches spiegeln die Struktur des Fachbereichs wider: Die drei parallelen Kurse sind durch die Farben orange, blau und grün gekennzeichnet.

Die vorgestellten Arbeiten befassen sich mit dem sensorischen Raum zwischen Realität und Virtualität.

105
Utopia
Bele Ducke >

chosen by contributing editor
Louise Sandhaus

complete work on the CD-ROM

Country >

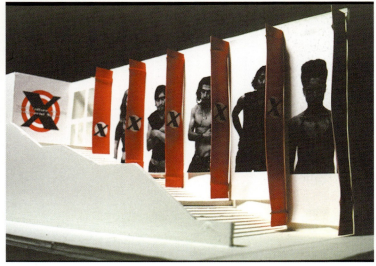

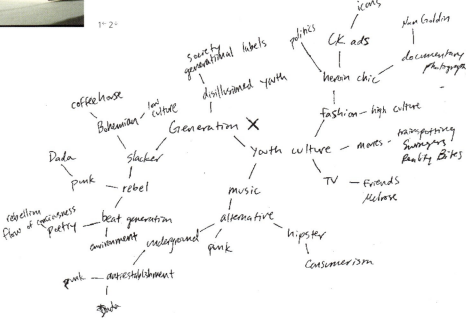

YOUTH CULTURE AND THE CONUSMERIST STATE

YOU WILL BE SHOWN:

- THE PRINCIPLES OF ANTIESTABLISHMENT ARTISTIC MOVEMENTS PLACED IN THE CONTEXT OF YOUTH ADVERTISING
- THE VISUAL LANGUAGE OF SOCIAL AND POLITICAL REBELLION USED AS A HIP AESTHETIC
- THE CONSTRUCTION OF A MYTHOLOGY OF THE "GENERATION X" SLACKER
- THE TRAGICALLY ROMANTIC APPEAL OF DISILLUSIONED YOUTH
- THE COMMODITY'S ASCENSION TO A SYMBOL OF IDENTITY
- CONSUMERISM AS A STATE IDEOLOGY CARRIED FORWARD THROUGH THE BRANDING OF YOUTH AS SOCIAL DEGENERATES

1	**Model for the Exhibition** *Modell der Ausstellung*
2	**Sketch** *Skizze*
3	**Poster for the Exhibition** *Ausstellungsplakat*
4	**Research: Calvin Klein** *Recherche: Calvin Klein*
5	**Research: OK Soda** *Recherche: OK Soda*
6	**Research: Nike** *Recherche: Nike*

THE OK. MANIFESTO

1. What's the point of "OK"? Well, what's the point of anything?
2. "OK" emphatically rejects anything that is not OK, and fully supports anything that is.
3. The better you understand something, the more OK it turns out to be.
4. "OK" Soda says, "Don't be fooled into thinking there has to be a reason for everything."
5. "OK" Soda reveals the surprising truth about people and situations.
6. "OK" Soda does not subscribe to any religion, or endorse any political party, or do anything other than feel OK.
7. "There is no real secret to feeling OK" --attributed to "OK" Soda, 1998.
8. "OK" may be the preferred drink of other people such as yourself.
9. Never overestimate the remarkable abilities of "OK."
10. Please wake up every morning knowing that things are going to be OK.

WHO THE HELL DOES NIKE THINK THEY ARE?

Youth culture and the comsumerist State
Jugendkultur im Konsumentenstaat

Dennis Gleason

Professor:
Katie Salen

College:
University of Texas at Austin

selected by the jury

Dennis Gleason:

The assignment was basically an exercise in exhibition design for an art gallery located on the ground floor at the entrance to our building. The students were asked to choose their own topic and imagine an exhibition of design works which represented the topic.

The topic for my exhibition was »Generation X advertising«.

The »culture industry« latched – after »Grunge Rock« – on a term used to describe the entire post-baby boom generation, and brandished it as a great new opportunity to label what had become a large, freely marketable target audience. The label is »Generation X« and the audience is a generation of desillusioned and rebellious twenty-somethings.

Recently, the heroin chic in fashion photography and advertising banked on the romanticism of being a down-and-out junkie addicted to the most glamorous and intensely rebellious of street drugs.

Die Aufgabe war ein Projekt im Bereich Ausstellungsdesign für eine Kunstgalerie im Erdgeschoß im Eingangsbereich unseres Gebäudes.

Die Studenten sollten ihr eigenes Thema wählen und sich eine Ausstellung von Designarbeiten ausdenken.

Das Thema für meine Ausstellung lautete: »Generation X Werbung«.

Nach dem »Grunge Rock« suchte die »Kulturindustrie« nach einem Begriff, der die Generation nach der der Babyboomer benennen sollte und zelebrierte ihn als eine große, neue Gelegenheit, das zu labeln, was zu einem großen, frei zu bewerbenden Zielpublikum herangewachsen war. Das Label »Generation X« und das Publikum sind eine Generation von desillusionierten und rebellischen Zwanzigjährigen.

Vor kurzem baute der Heroin-Chic in der Modefotografie und Werbung auf die romantisierte Vorstellung, ein ganz unten angekommener Junkie zu sein, der von der glamourösesten und rebellischsten Straßendroge abhängig ist.

Country

108

Heaven on Earth
CD ROM about the artists
Pierre and Gilles
Alle Herrlichkeit auf Erden
CD ROM über
das Künstlerpaar
Pierre und Gilles

< Iris Rütten +
Anke Schröder

Professor:
Klaus Mohr

College:
Fachhochschule Aachen

Study Year: 5

selected by the jury

complete work
on the CD-ROM

...provoking saints and pale graces, gentle slaves and untouched stars are dwelling in their sad glory and barbaric beauty. Gods drown in sweet bliss in the fragile, sugar glazed ambience ...

...reizende Heilige und blasse Grazien, zarte Sklaven und unberührte Stars schwelgen in ihrer traurigen Pracht und barbarischen Schönheit. Götter versinken in süßem Entzücken im zerbrechlichen Ambiente aus Zuckerguß...

< Country

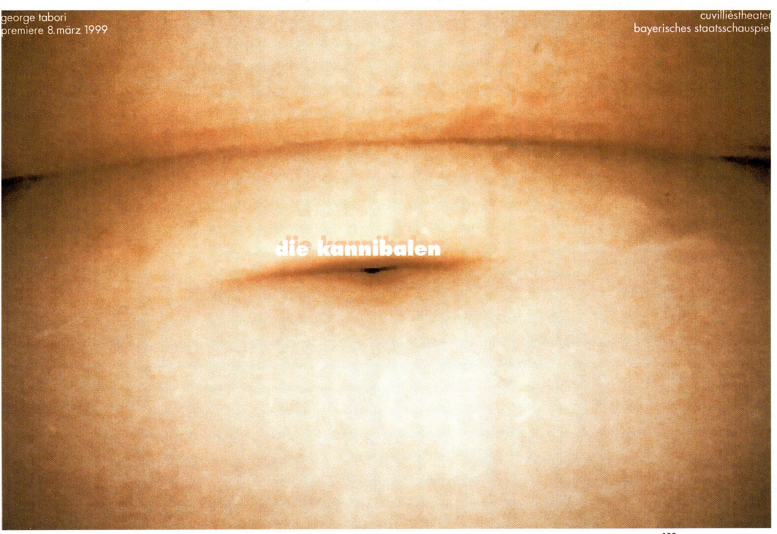

Poster for the theater play
»The Cannibals«
by George Tabori

Plakat für das Theaterstück
»Die Kannibalen«
von George Tabori

The Cannibals
Die Kannibalen

Annette Schmidt

Professor:
Judith Grieshaber

College:
Fachhochschule Konstanz

Study Year: 2

selected by the jury

Social campaign about the danger of Toxoplasm parasite for the human body. The series consists of: the cause (1), the effect (2, 3), how the infection can be spread (4, 5) and the prevention (6, 7).

Soziale Kampagne über die Gefahr der Toxoplasmose-Parasiten für den Menschen. Die Serie besteht aus: Ursache (1), Wirkung (2, 3), Übertragungswege (4, 5) und Vorbeugung (6, 7).

Campaign about the danger of Toxoplasm parasite
Kampagne über die Gefahren von Toxoplasmose-Parasiten

Poppy Yaneswari

Professor: Siti Turmini RZ
College: Jakarta Institute of Art
Study Year: 5

chosen by contributing editor Hanny Kardinata

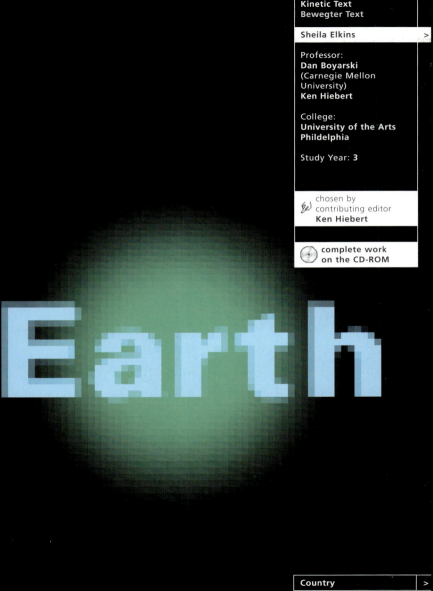

9 Tüten

»There is no better possibility
to experience life than
by walking down the street.«
Henry James

Pedestrian Zone
Fußgängerzone

< Katrin Schlüsener

Professor:
Prof. Pospischil

College:
Akademie der bildenden
Künste Stuttgart

Study Year: **4**

⊕ selected by the jury

»Es gibt keine bessere Möglichkeit das Leben zu erfahren,
als auf der Straße zu gehen.«
Henry James

< Country

113

Poster: Drugs

Juraj Balogh

Professor:
Radovan Jenko

College:
Academy of Fine Arts Ljubljana

Study Year: 4

selected by the jury

Country

Kelaynak türü göçmen kuşlarının
Ülkemizdeki yaşama alanları yokediliyor ve
avcıların bilinçsiz avlanması da
yokolmalarını hızlandırıyor.

irtibat hattı:230 30 20-230 40 40

caretta caretta

Caretta caretta denizkaplumbağalarının
nesli, Ülkemizdeki yaşama alanlarının
yokedilmesi yüzünden tehlike altında.

irtibat hattı:230 30 20-230 40 40

Fax Poster Campaign for the Society for Protection of Nature
Fax-Plakat-Kampagne für die Gesellschaft für Naturschutz

< **Bürkan Özkan**

Professor:
Yurdaer Altintas

College:
Mimar Sinan University Istanbul

chosen by contributing editor
Sadik Karamustafa

Fax Poster Campaign

These fax posters are designed to make people aware of the disappearing of endangering species such as Caretta Caretta Turtles, Mediterranean Seals and Kelaynak Birds. The campaign has been comissioned by the Society for the Protection of Nature. The posters will be send by fax to as many people as possible.

Diese Faxplakate wurden entworfen, um die Menschen auf bedrohte Tierarten aufmerksam zu machen, so z.B. die Caretta Caretta Schildkröten, die Mittelmeer-Robben und Kelaynak-Vögel. Die Kampagne wurde von der »Society for the Protection of Nature« in Auftrag gegeben. Die Plakate werden per Fax an so viele Menschen wie möglich verschickt.

Akdeniz foku nun nesli tehlikede!
Oların yokolması insan neslinin
sonu demektir.

irtibat hattı:230 30 20-230 40 40

OCVR (Optical Character Virtual Reality) is one of a series of typographic experiments by Micah Hahn addressing typography in digital realms. OCVR addresses the use and function of typography in immersive virtual environments. In conventional reading environments, readers encounter words on a flat two-dimensional surface; in immersive virtual environments there are no surfaces — readers must encounter words within space and through proximity. OCVR uses the principles of projective geometry to tie the location of the reader in space to legibilty. Words become intelligible only when the reader is located in the appropriate location within in the immersive environment, otherwise all the reader sees is an abstract galaxy of spheres.

The presentation of the project is comprised of two parts: Construction Area and View Movie. The Construction Area shows the information that makes up each character; View Movie offers a demo of a reader experience.

OCVR (Optical Character Virtual Reality) ist Teil einer Serie typographischer Experimente von Micah Hahn, die sich mit der Typographie in digitalen Welten befaßt. OCVR handelt vom Gebrauch und der Funktion der Typographie in tiefen, virtuellen Umgebungen. In konventionellen Leseumgebungen begegnen die Leser den Worten auf einer flachen, zweidimensionalen Oberfläche; in tiefen, virtuellen Umgebungen gibt es keine Oberflächen – die Leser müssen den Worten im Raum und durch Annäherung begegnen. OCVR benutzt die Prinzipien der projektiven Geometrie, um den Standort des Lesers im Raum mit der Lesbarkeit zu verbinden. Wörter werden nur dann verständlich, wenn der Leser sich an der entsprechenden Stelle in der tiefen Umgebung befindet, ansonsten sieht er lediglich eine abstrakte Galaxie aus Kugeln.

Die Präsentation des Projekts besteht aus zwei Teilen: dem Konstruktionsbereich und dem Filmvorführbereich (Construction Area und View Movie). Der Konstruktionsbereich zeigt die Information, die jeden Buchstaben zusammensetzt; der Filmvorführungsbereich zeigt eine Demonstration einer Lesererfahrung.

115

OCVR

Micah Hahn

Instructors:
Jeff Keedy,
Lorraine Wild,
Michael Worthington

College:
California Institute of Arts

Study Year:
1

chosen by contributing editor
Louise Sandhaus

complete work on the CD-ROM

Country

light to make

Maak

116

out of the dark

< **Christoph Kerschner**

🔍 selected by the jury

💿 complete work on the CD-ROM

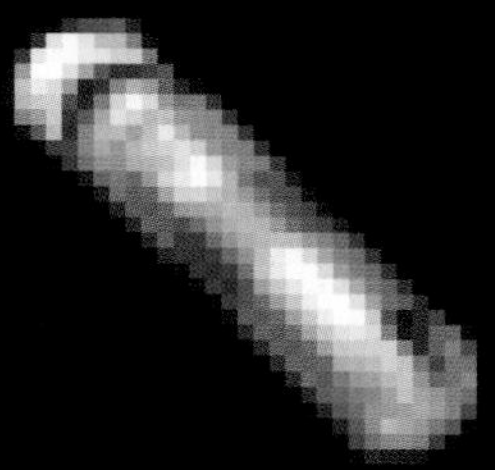

< Country

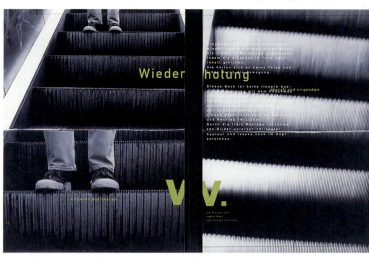

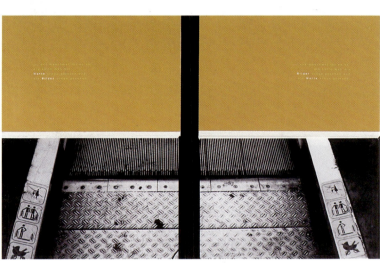

Judith Hehl
Carsten Hermann:

Repetition
Experimental book project on the subject of repetitions.
This book is not a linear confrontation with the phenomenon of repetitions. It has neither a beginning nor an end and should be read and seen in the most varying directions and perspectives. The left is repeated in the right and the right in the left. Through the free assembly, images melt and evoke new images in our minds.

Wiederholung –
experimentelles Buchobjekt zum Thema Wiederholungen.
Dieses Buch ist keine lineare Auseinandersetzung mit dem Phänomen der Wiederholung. Es hat weder Anfang noch Ende und will in unterschiedlichster Richtung gelesen und gesehen werden. Linkes wiederholt sich im Rechten und Rechtes im Linken. Durch die freie Montage verschmelzen Bilder und lassen neue im Kopf entstehen.

117

Repetition
Wiederholung

Judith Hehl +
Carsten Hermann

Professor:
Gerhard Schneider

College:
Fachhochschule
Darmstadt

selected by the jury

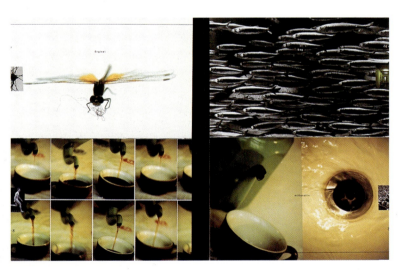
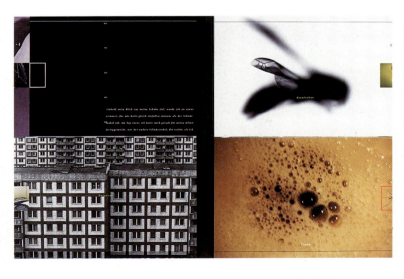

MetaDesign

Sehen Sie den Unterschied?

Corporate Identity
Webdesign
Branding
Intranet
Produktdesign
Interface Design
Corporate Design
Extranet
Kommunikationsdesign
Klärung
Internet
Industriedesign
Strategische Beratung
Marketingberatung
Konzepte
Logoentwicklung
Prozeßmethodik
Typosysteme
Informationstechnologie
Implementierung
Corporate Clothing
Softwareentwicklung
Dokumentationssysteme
Service
Pflege

MetaDesign Berlin
Bergmannstrasse 102
D-10961 Berlin
+49·30·695 79·200
fax +49·30·695 79·222
contact@metadesign.de
www.metadesign.de

Photography experimenting on the concept of time in still photography. The image represents the journey across a pedestrian suspension bridge.

Fotografie, die mit der Zeit in der unbewegten Fotografie experimentiert. Das Bild zeigt eine Reise über eine Fußgänger-Hängebrücke.

120 | **121**

Time in Photography
Zeit in der Fotografie

Michael Pollard

Professor:
Neil Grant
Dr. Eric Northey
Stephen Raw

College:
Manchester Metropolitain University

chosen by contributing editor
Neil Grant

Country

Ken Hiebert:

The project aquaints students with a musical language and culture foreign to them. Reserach consists of studies of actual rocks as a source for form and colour, the musical scores of Takemitsu, emaki painting style and Japanese Gardens which influenced Takemitsu, the clarinet, the solo instrument in this recording, and studies in the spatial placement of letter forms on 3-dimensional objects. It requires the integration of given informational text and functional requirements of CD use.

Das Projekt macht Studenten mit einer musikalischen Sprache und Kultur bekannt, die ihnen fremd ist. Die Recherche umfaßt die Untersuchung von echten Steinen als Quelle für Form und Farbe, die Partituren von Takemitsu, Emaki-Malerei und japanische Gärten, die Takemitsu beeinflußten, die Klarinette – das Soloinstrument in dieser Aufnahme – sowie Studien zu der räumlichen Anordnung von Buchstabenformen auf dreidimensionalen Objekten. Das Projekt erfordert die Integration von vorgegebenen Texten und funktionellen Voraussetzungen einer CD.

122

CD Package Design for works by Toru Takemitsu
Cover für eine Musik-CD von Toru Takemitsu

Mindi Tirabassi

Professor:
Ken Hiebert

College:
The University of the Arts Philadelphia

Study Year: 3

chosen by contributing editor
Ken Hiebert

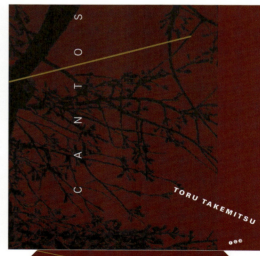

Country

1 Dividers for a file-card box with information material for the library staff to support the campagne
Zwischenblätter für einen Karteikasten, der Informationsmaterial für Mitarbeiter von Büchereien enthält zur Unterstützung der Kampagne

2 Posters for Libraries
Plakate für Büchereien

»New Ways to Read« is a campaign proposed by the Royal National Institute for the Blind within an overall theme being »Share the Vision« to help visually impaired people who would like to read.

The campaign was to provide information and practical support to libraries so that their stuff feel in a position to offer a good service to visually impaired customers and to allow individual libraries to select material which is appropriate to their special circumstances.

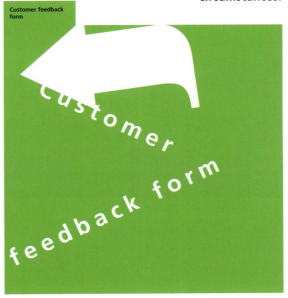

← ↑ 1

»New Ways to Read« ist eine vom »Royal National Institute for the Blind« vorgeschlagene Kampagne innerhalb des Hauptthemas »Share The Vision«, um sehbehinderte Menschen, die gerne lesen möchten, zu unterstützen.

Die Kampagne soll Büchereien Informationen und praktische Unterstützung bieten, damit das Personal sehbehinderten Kunden einen guten Service anbieten kann. Einzelne Büchereien können Material auswählen, das auf die besonderen Umstände dieser Kunden zugeschnitten ist.

123

New Ways to Read

Taline Yozgatian >

Professor:
Peter Rea
John Kortbawi

College:
Notre Dame University
Beirut

Study Year: **3**

🔍 selected by the jury

2 ↓

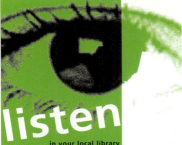  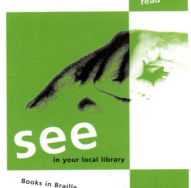

Country >

Lars Müller:

Briefing on the subject »science and communication«:
Formulate a statement on the current situation of (natural) science.

Visualize your statement.

The form and carrier for your work are free and depend upon practical criteria.

Meike Becker
Laurent Lacour:
Our main concern is not to communicate complicated facts but to make the principle of »science« accessible.

The photo sequences are metaphors for processes of research and scientific work. The motives are taken from the world of every-day life and experience. They are to be understandable for laymen and are in and of themselves only spacers that clarify a system of possible processes.

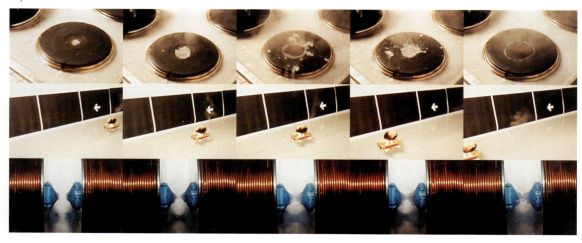

Ideal:
It is the simplest and most comfortable process of researching if everything the scientist X presumes as a possible process and result is then also proven to be correct.

Coincidence:
But many paths lead towards the goal. The irrational can also direct research onto new paths. The trial and error method can, for example, have the result that the presumption is abandoned and a new approach taken.

Vision:
The researcher will often consider a vague presumption, a vision of his or her goal to be something constant, and will work towards it. To what extent this vision will prove correct is in the stars.

1 Ideal

2 Coincidence
   Zufall

3 Vision

Lars Müller:

Briefing zum Thema »Wissenschaft und Kommunikation«:
Formulieren Sie eine Aussage zur gegenwärtigen Situation der (Natur-)wissenschaften.

Visualisieren Sie Ihre Aussage.

Form und Träger Ihrer Arbeit sind frei und richten sich nach praktischen Kriterien.

Meike Becker
Laurent Lacour:

Unser Hauptanliegen ist es nicht, komplizierte Sachverhalte zu vermitteln, sondern das Prinzip »Wissenschaft« näherzubringen.

Die Fotosequenzen sind Metaphern für Abläufe des Forschens und wissenschaftlichen Arbeitens. Die Motive entstammen dabei der Alltags- und Erfahrungswelt. Sie sollen auch für Nicht-Wissenschaftler nachvollziehbar sein und sind für sich genommen nur Platzhalter, die ein System von möglichen Abläufen veranschaulichen.

Ideal:
Der einfachste und angenehmste Verlauf des Forschens ist es, daß alles, was der Wissenschaftler X als denkbaren Verlauf und Ergebnis annimmt, auch genauso eintrifft.

Zufall:
Doch viele Wege führen zum Ziel. Auch das Irrationale kann Forschung in neue Bahnen lenken. Die »Try and Error«-Methode kann zum Beispiel das Ergebnis haben, daß das zuvor angenommene verworfen und ein neuer Ansatz gestartet wird.

Vision:
Oft wird der Forscher eine vage Annahme, eine Vision seines Ziels als etwas Konstantes betrachten und darauf zuarbeiten. Wie weit sich seine Vision dann als richtig erweist, steht in den Sternen.

124 | **125**

Ideal – Coincidence – Vision:
15 photographic sequences which describe possible processes of research and scientific work
Ideal – Zufall – Vision:
15 Fotosequenzen, die metaphorisch mögliche Handlungsabläufe des Forschens und wissenschaftlichen Arbeitens beschreiben

**Meike Becker +
Laurent Lacour**

Professor:
Lars Müller

College:
Hochschule für Gestaltung Offenbach

Study Year: **5**

selected by the jury

Country

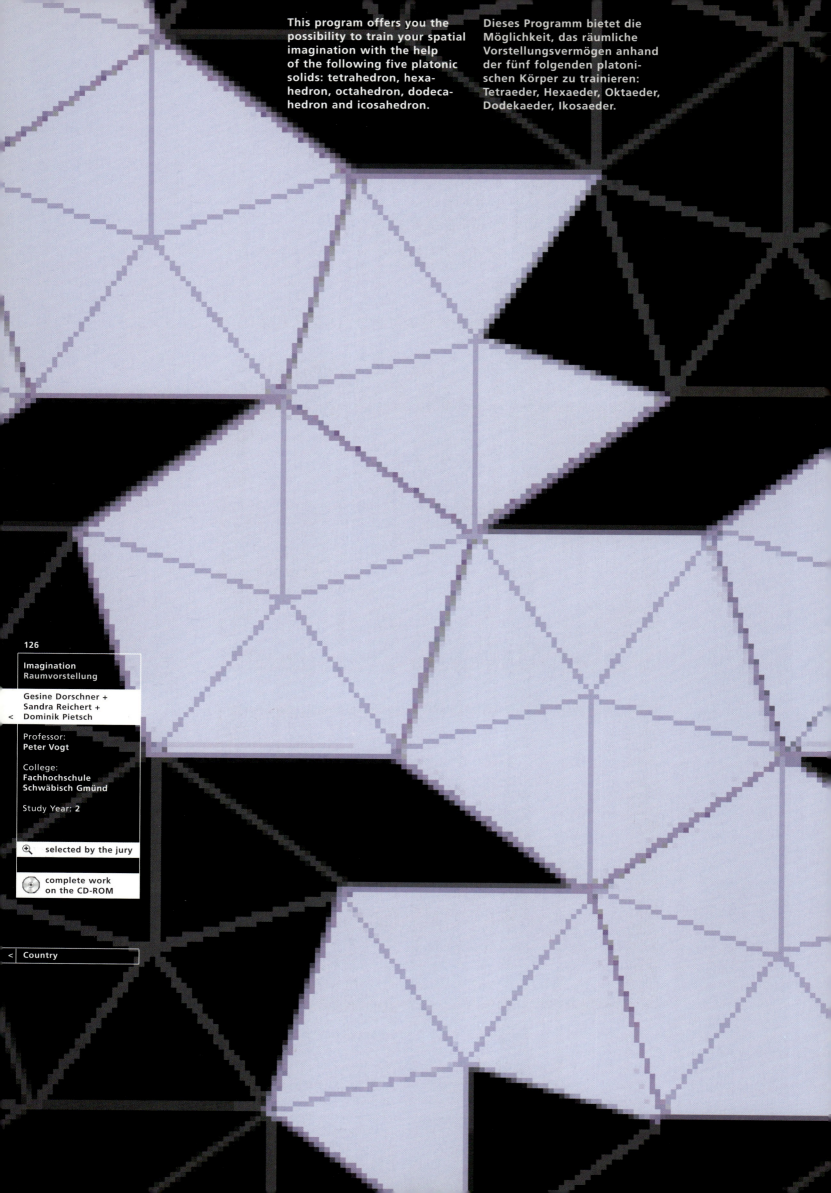

This program offers you the possibility to train your spatial imagination with the help of the following five platonic solids: tetrahedron, hexahedron, octahedron, dodecahedron and icosahedron.

Dieses Programm bietet die Möglichkeit, das räumliche Vorstellungsvermögen anhand der fünf folgenden platonischen Körper zu trainieren: Tetraeder, Hexaeder, Oktaeder, Dodekaeder, Ikosaeder.

Imagination
Raumvorstellung

Gesine Dorschner +
Sandra Reichert +
< Dominik Pietsch

Professor:
Peter Vogt

College:
Fachhochschule
Schwäbisch Gmünd

Study Year: 2

selected by the jury

complete work on the CD-ROM

< Country

Identity for a TV Station
Erscheinungsbild für einen Fernsehsender

Isil Döneray

Professor:
Bülent Erkmen

College:
Mimar Sinan University of Arts, Istanbul

selected by the jury

Poster series
Visual flight towards aesthetics

(1) Life in the cities is marked by overcrowded streets. The view from apartment windows catches uniform concrete dwellings. In this overcrowded environment people have too little room for movement. They indulge in consumption to satisfy their inner needs. They take a visual flight into aesthetics.

(2) We can only perceive a small part of the world sharply in our field of vision. This angle of vision is about 1 to 2 degrees. This natural restriction of the field of vision makes it easy for people to overlook what they don't like.

(3) The lack in gestalt in the cities causes people to devote themselves to the aestheticising of trivial matters. A color combination or an otherwise unnoticed tool achieves a formal aesthetic.

(4) People select from their environment that which contains information relevant for them.

Plakatserie
Visuelle Flucht zur Ästhetik

(1) Das Leben in Städten ist von überfüllten Straßen geprägt. Der Blick aus Wohnungsfenstern fällt auf Einheitsbehausungen aus Beton. In dieser überfüllten Umwelt bleibt den Menschen zu wenig Bewegungsspielraum. Sie stürzen sich in den Konsum, um ihre inneren Bedürfnisse zu befriedigen. Sie begehen eine visuelle Flucht zur Ästhetik.

(2) Von der Welt, die sich in unserem Gesichtsfeld befindet, können wir nur einen kleinen Teil scharf sehen. Dieser Sehwinkel beträgt etwa 1-2 Grad. Diese natürliche Einschränkung des Gesichtsfeldes macht es den Menschen leicht, unliebsames einfach zu übersehen.

(3) Die Gestaltlosigkeit der Städte veranlaßt die Menschen, sich der Ästhetisierung banaler Dinge zu widmen. Eine Farbkombination oder ein sonst unbeachtetes Gerät erreicht formale Ästhetik.

(4) Die Menschen suchen sich aus ihrer Umgebung denjenigen Teil heraus, der für sie relevante Informationen enthält.

Visual flight towards aesthetics
Visuelle Flucht zur Ästhetik

Jochen Tratz

Professor:
Ulrich Braun

College:
Fachhochschule Würzburg

Study Year: 5

selected by the jury

Country

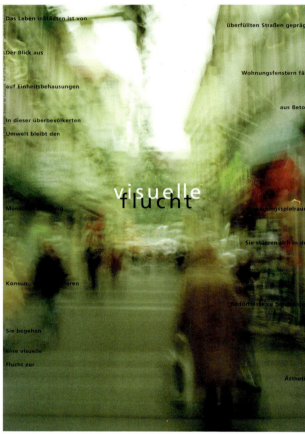

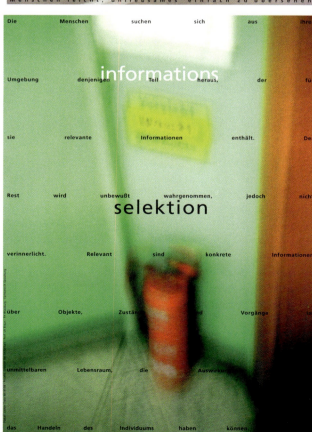

Extreme contrasts of color and brightness can deceive the human eye. With interactive examples, this work demonstrates optical phenomena and deceptions such as simultaneous contrast, Moirée effect and after-images.

Extreme Farb- und Helligkeitskontraste können das menschliche Auge in die Irre führen. Anhand von interaktiven Beispielen werden in dieser Arbeit optische Phänomene und Täuschungen wie Simultankontrast, Moirée-Effekt und Nachbilder anschaulich gemacht.

129

Optical Phenomena
Optische Phänomene

Professor:
Prof. Reinke
Prof. Vogt

Petra Sutter
Annika Kaltenthaler

College:
Fachhochschule Schwäbisch Gmünd

selected by the jury

complete work on the CD-ROM

Country

Eduardo Cortada Hindersin

Prof. José Baltanás

Red Paralela is the result of research work developed as a final year project. It is a personal proposal, the motivation of which comes from the social ignorance of the cultural activities promoted by minority groups that are hardly interconnected. The objectives of the project are:

(1) To create a global visual identity that gives an entity to this cultural offer.

(2) To design an information system that marks in conceptual and graphical ways this specific alternative offer.

(3) To facilitate a quick distribution, interconnected and with a low cost.

The research for this project was no easy task given the fact that the information was very homogeneous: the different cultural groups that don't belong to the official cultural circles of Barcelona are spread throughout the city.

The work suggests – with a great amount of poetry – uniting this alternative, unofficial, constantly changing culture in a container (pic. 1) representing a common house whose interior provides room for a large number of various activities, groups and cultural experiences.

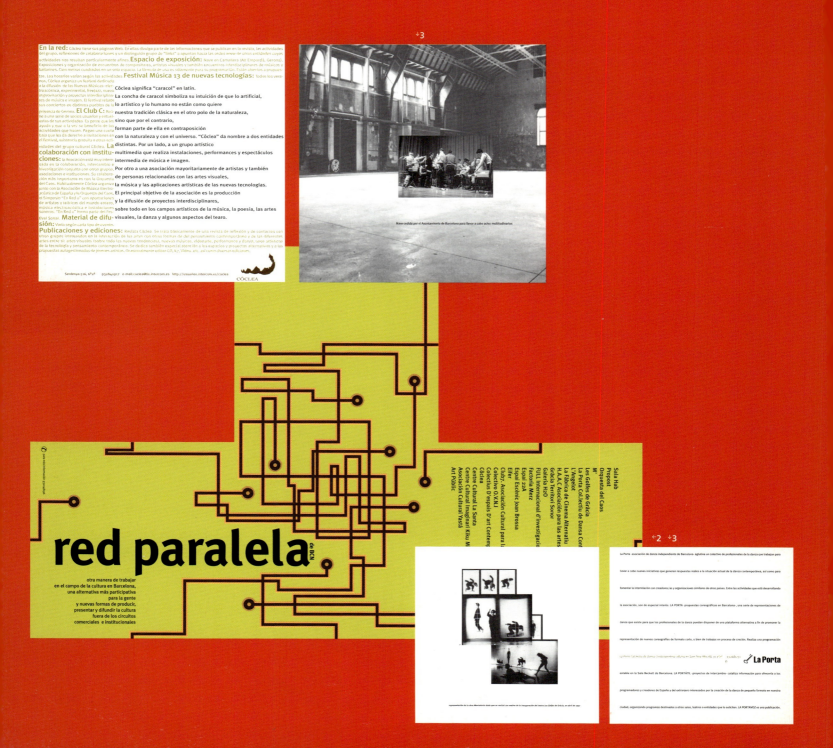

1 Container to collect
information material
Karton zum Aufbewahren
von Informationsmaterial

2 Posters
Plakate

3 Informations about
cultural events
Informationsblätter
für kulturelle
Veranstaltungen

Eduardo Cortada Hindersin (Student):

Red Paralela ist das Ergebnis einer Recherche, die als Abschlußprojekt weiterentwickelt wurde. Es ist ein persönlicher Ansatz, dessen Motivation aus der Ignoranz gegenüber alternativen, kulturellen Aktivitäten stammt, die von Minderheiten betrieben werden.

Die Ziele des Projektes sind:

(1) Der Entwurf einer visuellen Identität, die diesem kulturellen Angebot eine Einheit verleiht.

(2) Das Design eines Informationssystems, das konzeptionell und grafisch dieses alternative Angebot kennzeichnet.

(3) Die Erleichterung der schnellen Verbreitung zu geringen Kosten.

Prof. José Baltanás (Professor):

Die Recherche für dieses Projekt war keine leichte Aufgabe angesichts der Tatsache, daß die Informationen sehr homogen waren: Die unterschiedlichen kulturellen Gruppen, die nicht zu den offiziellen Kulturzirkeln von Barcelona gehören, sind über die gesamte Stadt verteilt.

Die Arbeit schlägt vor – mit einem großen Maß an Poesie –, diese alternative, inoffizielle, sich ständig verändernde Kultur in Barcelona in einem Behälter (Abb. 1) zusammenzufassen, der ein gemeinsames Haus darstellt, dessen Inneres eine große Zahl unterschiedlicher Aktivitäten, Gruppen und kulturellen Erfahrungen beherbergt.

Red Paralela

Eduardo Cortada Hindersein

Professor:
Lluis Lannes
José Baltanás

College:
ESDI – Escola Superior de Disseny, Barcelona

Study Year: 4

selected by the jury

Country

Antje Schnier:

Umfragen zufolge sind Jugendliche heute schneller zu Gewalt und Risiko bereit als jemals zuvor. Erwachsene haben kaum mehr Zutritt zu deren Lebensräumen. Eine Kampagne gegen Gewaltbereitschaft unter Jugendlichen muß sich also anderer Mittel bedienen als herkömmliche Kommunikationskonzepte.

Ein unter Jugendlichen weit verbreitetes Medium sind Flyer. Sie haben den Vorteil, daß sie klein sind, jederzeit in die Tasche gesteckt werden können und oftmals zu Sammelobjekten werden.

Die Flyer sind mit Fotokopien und Siebdruck hergestellt. Die verwendete Schrift Arial ist für jeden Schüler verfügbar. So kann die Kampagne von jedem aufgenommen und weitergeführt werden.

Antje Schnier

According to surveys, young people are more amenable towards violence and risk-taking today than ever before. Adults hardly have any more access to their living environments. A campaign against the will for violence among young people therefore has to use means other than traditional communication concepts.

132

Underground campaign against violence amongst teenagers
Untergrundkampagne gegen Gewalt unter Jugendlichen

Professor:
Silke Juchter

< Antje Schnier +
Monika Waigand

College:
Muthesius Hochschule Kiel

Study Year: 3

selected by the jury

Flyers are a widespread medium among young people. They have the advantage of being small; they can be put into a pocket at any time and often become collectibles.

The flyers were made with photocopies and silk screening. The font that was used, Arial, is available to every pupil. The campaign can thus be taken up and continued by everybody.

< Country

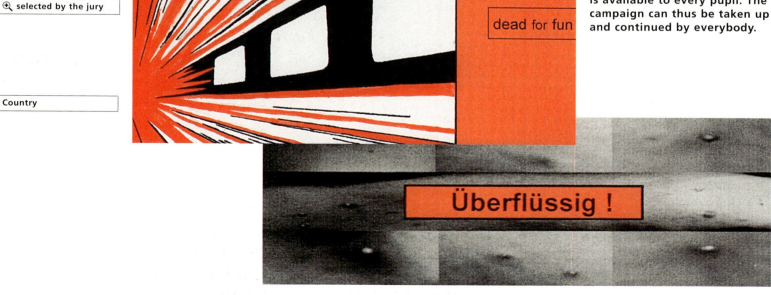

Silke Eggers:

Advertising surrounds us and is constantly present. The marketing of products in advertising embodies, first of all, their image and sell dream worlds (brand image).

Uncountable clichés from the perfect career woman and mother to the ideal young and dynamic scene type are being used. Young people, especially, are influenced by these examples of happiness. The attempt to live up to the various images often leads to failure and disappointment.

My campaign is an information campaign. Through urgent imagery, the observer's attention is awakened and motivated to deal with it.

DAS LEBEN IST FÜR MICH EIN TANZ, ALLES EINE FRAGE DER BALANCE.
glatt gelogen

ICH BIN AKTIV DEN GANZEN TAG, SO VIEL AROMA.
glatt gelogen

FÜR DAS BESTE IM MANN.
glatt gelogen

Campaign against the illusion of a perfect world in commercials
Kampagne gegen die heile Welt in der Werbung

Silke Eggers

Professor:
Silke Juchter

College:
Muthesius Hochschule Kiel

Study Year: 4

selected by the jury

Country

Silke Eggers:

Werbung ist überall um uns herum und ständig präsent. Produkte in der Werbung verkörpern in erster Linie ihr Image und verkaufen Traumwelten (Markenimage). Dabei werden unzählige Klischees von der perfekten Karrierefrau und Mutter bis zum idealen jung-dynamischen Szenetypen bedient. Besonders junge Menschen sind von diesem vorgelebten Glück beeinflußt. Der Versuch den verschiedenen Images zu entsprechen führt oft zum Scheitern und zur Enttäuschung.

Meine Kampagne ist eine Aufklärungskampagne. Der Betrachter wird aufmerksam gemacht und durch eine eindringliche Bildsprache zur Auseinandersetzung angeregt.

Paper Promotion introducing Asmat culture (one of Indonesian ethnic groups living in Iria Jaya)
Papier-Promotion, die die Asmat Kultur vorstellt (eine indonesische Volksgruppe aus Irian Jaya)

Bambang Irawan

Professor:
Yongky Safanayong

College:
Universita Pelita Harapan Jakarta

Study Year: 3

chosen by contributing editor
Hanny Kardinata

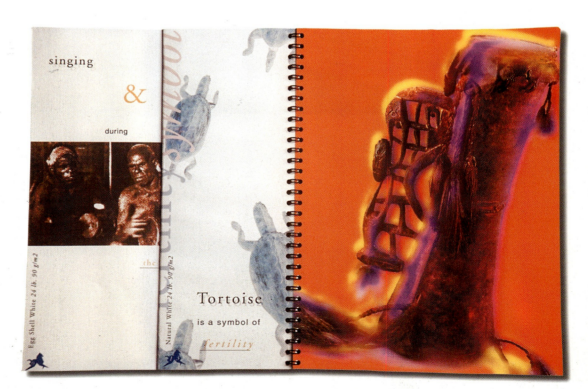

Die Web Site »out there« wurde gestaltet um ein Design-Projekt zu unterstützen, das in Zusammenarbeit mit der Gemeinde von Liverpool entwickelt wurde.

»out there« war in das Projekt integriert und unterstützte den Entwurfsprozeß in allen relevanten Phasen, wie zum Beispiel Recherche, Dialog und Austausch, Anfertigung von Skizzen, Produktion und Post-Produktion.

Materialien der Online-Recherche (Artikel, Web sites, Briefings, Zeitpläne, Karten, Informationen über die Gemeinde und mit dem Projekt zusammenhängende Daten) wurden direkt auf der Website gespeichert und konnten dort von den Studenten abgerufen und ausgetauscht werden.

Die Dynamik des Verhältnisses »Lehrer sendet, Schüler empfängt« war aufgebrochen, zum Teil, weil die Diskussion und die gemeinsame Nutzung von Daten in das Projekt integriert war.

feedback welcomed!

The web site »out there« was developed to support a public design project with the Liverpool community.

Out there was integrated into the coursework of the Liverpool project and content was directly informed by the subject needs. The website content was designed to meet the design process and the relevant production phases. research, ongoing dialogue and exchange, draft designs, production and post-production.

Online research materials - journal articles, web sites, project brief, timeline, Liverpool neighbourhood plan, background material on the community and related works (texts and www) were posted to the site at the commencement of the project and students enjoyed being able to share research findings in the initial phase of the project.

The dynamic of teacher delivers/students receive was broken down, particularly because peer critiquing and shared project resourcing was integrated into the coursework.

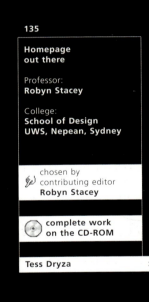

135

Homepage
out there

Professor:
Robyn Stacey

College:
School of Design
UWS, Nepean, Sydney

chosen by
contributing editor
Robyn Stacey

complete work
on the CD-ROM

Tess Dryza >

Country >

:AIDS: DAS IMMUNSYSTEM IST WIE UNSER ALPHABET. WIR HABEN IN UNSEREM ALPHABET HÄUFIG VORKOMMENDE BUCHSTABEN, ZUM BEISPIEL DIE VOKALE, UND SELTENE, WIE DIE KONSONANTEN, Y ZUM BEISPIEL. WENN DU NUN IN DEINER SPRACHE DAS Y VERLIERST, DANN IST DAS KEIN GROSSES PROBLEM. WIRST DU DAS Q VERLIEREN, DANN KANNST DU DAMIT AUCH NOCH LEBEN. WENN ABER EINMAL DAS E ODER DAS WEGFALLEN, WIRD ES SCHWER. DAS HEISST, JEDEN TAG, AN DEM DAS VIRUS ZEIT HAT, IM KÖRPER ZERSTÖRUNGEN ANZURICHTEN, WIRD ES AUCH IMMUNOLOGISCHE BUCHSTABEN ERSTÖREN. IRGEND ANN SIND DANN IELLEICHT EINMAL ALLE EG – MACHT NI – ABER IRGEND ANN ERSCH INDEN DANN IELLEICH ALLE E ND DANN BEKOMMEN IR SCH IERIGKEI EN. DIE MEDI INI CHE BE EB NG I N N, DA IMM N EM I GEND O AN EINEM NK E I CHEN, AN DEM D N CH FA DEIN GAN E AL HABE HA DE MINDE DANN, ENN D CH DIE ICH IG E B CHABE HA . D DA DA IEDE DIE E GE CHICHE: E D E 250, 200 E FE E E I , C IE DI DA I IE EIC E A DE E E E A A , DA E E DA E A A D C E E , DA C A , DA C C A , DA B A A C . A A A , AB A , A A ?

»Vor 12 Jahren wurde mein Lebenspartner Ernst ohne sein Wissen getestet. Ergebnis: HIV positiv. Als Nicht-Infizierter fühlte ich mich verbindlich »mit« betroffen. Seitdem kämpfen wir gemeinsam gegen diese Bedrohung. Die ersten Freunde sind erkrankt. Die ersten Freunde sind qualvoll gestorben. Andere liegen im Sterben – eine Frage der Zeit. Wir haben uns daran gewöhnt, uns auf Friedhöfen zu begegnen. Abschied zu nehmen. Wir haben unsere Unbefangenheit verloren.

Ich registriere den Verlauf dieser unberechenbaren Krankheit. Ich berichte über Menschen, die dem verfrühten Sterben nicht gewachsen sind. Die, die darüberhinaus auch noch der gesellschaftlichen Ächtung ausgesetzt sind.

Ich bin Menschen begegnet, die ihren Lebenspartner verlassen haben. Endgültig.

Ich bin aber auch Menschen begegnet, die – um ihrem Lebenspartner Geborgenheit zu vermitteln – über sich hinausgewachsen sind.

Die Chance über uns hinauszuwachsen, haben wir die nicht alle?«

Christian Noak, Kahlschlag, Versuch einer Bewältigung, 1997

»12 years ago, my partner, Ernst, was tested without his knowledge. Result: HIV positive. As a non-infected person, I obligatorily felt concerned. Since then we've been fighting against this threat. The first friends have fallen ill. The first friends have died miserably. Others are dying – it's only a question of time. We have gotten used to meeting in cemeteries, bidding farewell. We have lost our innocence. I register the course of this incalculable disease. I report about people who can't handle dying so early in life. Those who are, beyond this, subject to the ostracism of society. I have met people who have left their partners. For good.

But I also met people who have grown beyond themselves in order to give their partner comfort.

Don't we all have the opportunity to grow beyond ourselves?«

Christian Noak, Kahlschlag, Versuch einer Bewältigung, 1997

136 | 137

Positive

Professor:
Prof. Pocock
Prof. Sommer

Ellen Schweizer >

College:
Fachhochschule Pforzheim

Study Year: 4

selected by the jury

Country >

In einer ungewöhnlichen und innovativen Form treffen in dem Buch »Kultur des Friedens« Texte und Bilder zum Thema Frieden und Unfrieden aufeinander. Auf 512 Seiten stellen über 50 ausgewiesene Friedens- und Zukunftsforscher in 48 wissenschaftlichen Texten Möglichkeiten, Aussichten und Perspektiven einer Friedenskultur vor. Die Texte werden mit über 500 Bildern von 59 zum Teil international renommierten, vielfach ausgezeichneten Fotografen, Gestaltern, Illustratoren und Künstlern aus dem In- und Ausland konfrontiert, die die Projektgruppe Unesco-Buch zur honorarfreien Mitarbeit gewinnen konnte. Es entsteht Spannung zwischen wissenschaftlicher Analyse und künstlerischen Fragestellungen.

Das Buch ist ein Beitrag zum UNESCO-Programm »Culture of Peace« und der Unesco zum 50jährigen Bestehen gewidmet.

In the book »Culture of Peace«, texts and images on the subject of peace and discord come together in an unusual and innovative form. On 512 pages, over 50 renowned peace and futurist researchers present the possibilities, outlooks and perspectives of a peace culture in 48 scientific texts. The texts are supplemented with over 500 images by 59 photographers, some internationally renowned and honored, designers, illustrators and artists from home and abroad who were willing to collaborate with the project group no fee. A tension between scientific analysis and artistic questioning is created.
The book is a contribution to the UNESCO program »Culture of Peace« and dedicated to Unesco for its 50th anniversary.

138 | 139

Culture of Peace
Kultur des Friedens

Professor:
Eckhard Jung

College:
Hochschule für Künste Bremen

Nikolai Wolff +
Sebastian Bissinger

chosen by contributing editor
Eckhard Jung

Country

The bus map for Beirut works bilingual. On the right side one can find the english version and on the left side the arabic version. The english stop chart covers the arabic map (sketch) and the other way round.

Der Busfahrplan für Beirut ist zweisprachig aufgebaut. Rechts befindet sich der englische und links der arabische Text. Die Legende deckt den jeweils anderssprachigen Plan ab (Skizze).

Map for the Beirut public transport system
Busfahrplan für Beirut

< Lara Chamoun

Professor:
Yara Khoury
Diane Mikhael

College:
Notre Dame University of Beirut, Lebanon

Study Year: **3**

chosen by contributing editor
Peter Rea

< Country

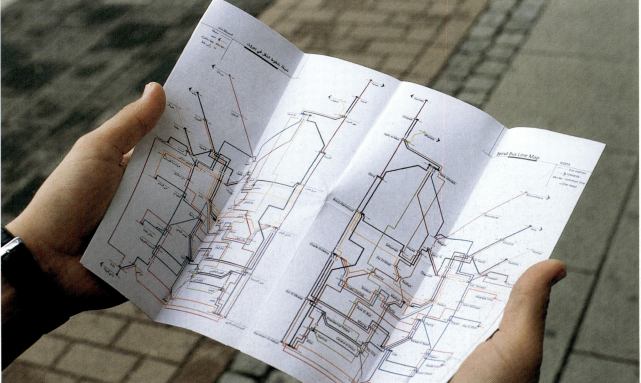

Idee
CD mit Originalklängen verschiedener Städte, die dem Zuhörer eine Audiotour durch städtische Umgebungen bietet.

Konzept
Als ich nach New York zog, wurde mir klar, wie verschieden und aufregend die Klänge verschiedener Städte sind und jeder Stadt ihren eigenen Charakter verleihen. Mir wurde auch klar, daß ihnen nicht genügend Beachtung geschenkt wird. In einer Stadt sind wir einer Vielzahl von Klängen ausgesetzt, die unser Bewußtsein und Unterbewußtsein beeinflussen. Die Stadtklang-CD bietet den Hörern die Möglichkeit, die urbane Umgebung auf diskrete und abstrakte Weise zu erleben. Das Hören der Klänge auf diese Art verändert unsere Wahrnehmung: Lärm wird zur Musik.

»Noise« reflektiert den wöchentlichen Rhythmus der Stadt, indem auf der CD Geräusche an unterschiedlichen Tagen und zu verschiedenen Tageszeiten aufgenommen wurden. Das Konzept begann in New York City und wird auf andere Städte übertragen.

Idea
CD of original ambient sounds of various cities which gives the listener an audio tour through urban environments.

Concept
When I moved to New York I realized how different and exciting the sounds of each city are, giving each city its own unique character. I also realized how they are underappreciated. Being in a city exposes us to multitude of sounds thbat influence our consciousness and subconsciousness. The city sound CD gives listeners the chance to experience the urban environment in a discreet and abstract way. Listening to these sounds in this format changes our perception: Noise becomes music.

Noise reflects the weekly rhythm of the city by capturing sounds in different days and time of day. The concept started in New York City and is continued to other cities.

141

Noise

Miriam Bossard

Professor:
Steven Guarnaccia

College:
School of Visual Arts
New York

chosen by contributing editor
Steven Heller

Country

pharmakologisch®

Mitleid ist der Biß ins Brot neben einem,
dem der Hunger den Bauch auftreibt wie einen
Ballon.
Brot mit Tränen gegessen ist würzig und nahrhaft,

es beruhigt die Nerven, es macht satt.

[Edel sei der Mensch, hilfreich und gut]

Wer kein Mitleid hat, ist kein Mensch.
Wer keine Tränen hat, ist kein Mensch.
Wer kein Brot hat, von dem er abbeißen kann,
wird über die Dächer fliegen.
Kinder werden den Finger aus dem Mund ziehen
und hinaufzeigen, bis der Ballon hinter der
verwaschenen Wetterseite der Apotheke
verschwunden ist.

Letzten Endes hat jedes Ding seinen Zweck.

[Es ist alles trefflich eingerichtet.]

Hilfreich ist der Ballon eines aufgetriebenen
Bauches.
Den edlen Brotessern zieht er den Kork aus der
Flasche
mit den guten Augentropfen:

Mitleid [commiseratio]
3 mal tägl. 2

Äußerlich!

```
HERUMKUGELN
EINFACH HERUMKUGELN      %6562
IST AUCH ETWAS.
                           ÖS

EIN KLEINER STEIN        *1.00
DER IRGENDWO LIEGT.      *1.00
ODER EIN ZERKNUELLTER    *1.00
ZETTEL:                  *1.00
DU MACHST IHN AUF        *1.00
UND ES STEHT NICHTS      *1.00
DRAUF AUSSER             *1.00
VIELLEICHT *7 SCHILLING*.
                          *0.7
DIESE RECHUNG WAR         *0.7
  0.924kg    3.99 kg
BILLIG.                  *00.7


                         ÖS.07
```

das schwein

erst sagen wollte ich: geliebtes tier
bei zweitem denken sage ich: beliebtes tier
das schwein ist ein beliebtes tier
lieblich wenn klein wenn älter mürrisch
jederzeit gut zu essen
der große bogen um den stier
wird um das schwein meist nicht geschlagen
ich bin bewegt von seinem schönen rüssel

Ernst Jandl

Students of the
College of Arts
Braunschweig

Professor:
Kornelia Becker

Typographic Interpretations
of poems of Ernst Jandl

Typografische Interpretationen
von Gedichten von Ernst Jandl

Students:
Matthias Klose
Matthias Langer
Monika Langrock
Nicole Lübnitz
Sven Rohde
Torsten Uhde
Dunlin Wilson

brille

alles in meinem kopf
ist oft nichts
außer ein flimmern
es fehlt der fokus

sich auf eine einzige
stelle zu konzentrieren
fehlt nicht der wille
sondern eine art brille

Deutsche Telekom T · · · · · Telegramm · 01A

▽ Name, Vorname (Firma)
▽ Straße, Hausnummer
▽ Gebäudeteil, Etage
▽ Postleitzahl ▽ Ort
▽ Land (nur Ausland)

Anfrage

▽ Blatt-Nr. 01
▽ von 01 (Gesamt)

Empfänger

Postleitzahl nicht vergessen !

▽ Referenz-Nr. (bitte nicht ausfüllen)

ICH SCHICKTE MEINEN NAMEN AUS DER STADT
IN TELEGRAMMEN, UND FUHR HINTERHER.
DER ZUG DER MICH HERAUSZOG AUS DER STADT
BLIEB IM GELEISE.
ICH SCHICKTE MEINEN NAMEN IN DIE STADT
IN TELEGRAMMEN, UND FUHR HINTERHER.
DER ZUG DER MICH ZURÜCKZOG IN DIE STADT
BLIEB IM GELEISE.
WO BLIEB DIE REISE ?

Kurz-telegramm

Telegramm-Text

▽ Name, Vorname (Firma) JANDL, ERNST
▽ Straße, Hausnummer WOHLLEBGASSE
▽ Postleitzahl ▽ Ort WIEN

Absender

▽ Ortsnetzkennzahl ▽ Telefon-Nummer

Ich wünsche die Zustellung

▽ durch Boten X	▽ auch nachts (bei Aufgabe nach 18.00 Uhr) X	▽ auf Schmuckblatt (LX ...)	▽ als Seefunk-telegramm	▽ Anzahl Kopien 01
▽ über Telefon	▽ über Telefax	▽ Ortsnetzkennzahl	▽ Rufnummer (linksbündig)	
▽ Dringend X	▽ Schmuckblatt	▽ Traueranlaß	Diese Angaben gelten nur bei Telegrammen in das Ausland!	

Zustellung

R+Co 2.96/2

▽ Sonstige Dienstvermerke (dieser Bereich ist nicht vom Kunden auszufüllen) ▽ Referenz-Nr. (bitte nicht ausfüllen)

01B ▽ Kassennummer ▽ JSNR ▽ Annahme-Datum ▽ Annahme-Uhrzeit

KN 937 200 000-6 / MN 17 003 226

144

100 Years Bertolt Brecht
100 Jahre Bertolt Brecht

Professor:
Anna Berkenbusch

College:
Universität Gesamthochschule Essen

< **Yvonne Günther + Christopher Wiehl**

selected by the jury

< Country

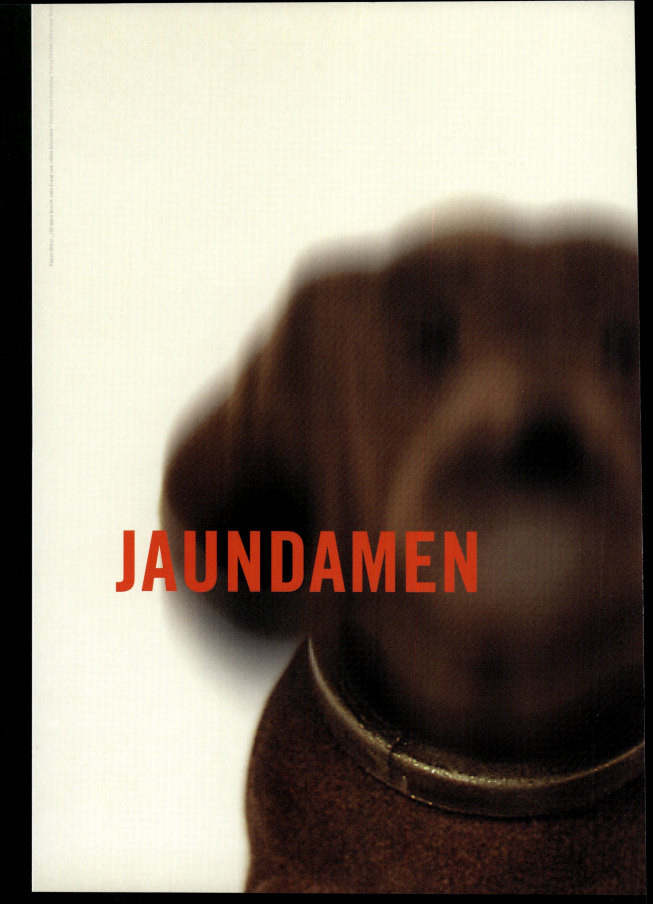

1↑

1+2
Brecht 100 Plakate –
internationale Plakataktion
veranstaltet vom Berliner
Ensemble und dem Verband der
Grafiker Deutschlands (VGD).

Insgesamt 100 internationale Designer und Hochschulen wurden angeschrieben, an der Plakataktion »100 Jahre Brecht, 100 Plakate« teilzunehmen. An den Hochschulen fand jeweils ein interner Wettbewerb statt, da nur ein Plakat eingereicht werden konnte.

1+2
Brecht 100 posters –
international poster action
organized by the Berlin Ensemble
and the Association of Graphic
Designers in Germany, VGD.

100 international designers and design colleges were asked to participate in the poster action »100 years of Brecht, 100 posters«. At the colleges, an internal competition was held since only one poster per school could be submitted.

3

Poster-leaflet
Plakat-Broschüre

2

Plakatausstellung

Aussagen zum Zustand der Welt.

Berliner Ensemble

Eröffnung: 10. Februar 1998, 18 Uhr

Mo. bis Fr., 10 bis 18 Uhr

10. Februar bis 17. März 1998

Bertolt Brecht ist 100 Jahre alt

145

100 Years Bertolt Brecht
100 Jahre Bertolt Brecht

Professor:
Anna Berkenbusch

College:
Universität Gesamthochschule Essen

Stefanie Saxe

selected by the jury

Country

*Neu: Lamy accent.
Das erste Schreibgerät mit
verschiedenen auswechselbaren
Griffstücken!*

Den Wunsch nach mehr Individualität erfüllt der LAMY accent auf innovative Art. Ist er doch das erste Schreibgerät, bei dem man ganz nach Geschmack unter verschiedenen austauschbaren Griffstücken wählen kann. Es gibt ihn als Füllhalter, Tintenschreiber, Kugelschreiber oder Druckbleistift. Palladium beschichtet oder in Mattschwarz. Von DM 69,– bis DM 99,–. Jedes zusätzliche Griffstück kostet DM 10,–. (Unverbindliche Preisempfehlungen) www.lamy.de

LAMY
Die Lust am Schreiben.

Juraj Klementin Balogh (113)
Ipelska 15
82107 Bratislava
Slovakia
fon +421 (0)7 43 42 16 17
b.juraj@mailcity.com

Sandra Baumer (88)
Thrasolt 7-9
D-10585 Berlin
fon +49 (0)173 2 09 56 79
designkantine@hotmail.com

Meike Becker (124)
Wittelsbacherallee 76
D-60385 Frankfurt/Main
fon +49 (0)69 44 29 75
laurent@stud.uni-frankfurt.de

Jürgen Bertram (74)
Viehofer Platz 2
D-45127 Essen
fon +49 (0)201 2 48 56 20
j_bert@topmail.de

Gabriele Berueter (62)
Hohlstr. 210
CH-8004 Zürich
Switzerland
fon +41 (0)1 2 91 56 50

Sebastian Bissinger (138)
Ostertorsteinweg 1-2
D-28203 Bremen
fon +49 (0)421 7 94 81 36

Miriam Bossard (141)
169 E. Broadway #20
New York, NY 10002
USA
fon +1 212 2 28 12 07
mbossard@student.schoolofvisualarts.edu

Christiane Bruckmann (35, 58)
Hamburger Berg 25
D-20359 Hamburg
fon/fax +49 (0)40 31 79 41 02
tjane@rrz.uni-hamburg.de

Bettina Bruder (54)
Poppenweilerstr. 25
D-70439 Stuttgart
fon/fax +49 (0)711 80 75 81
benzinablond@hotmail.com

Heike Burkhardt (99)
Birkenstr. 30
D-28816 Stuhr
fon +49 (0)421 80 80 30

Anders Carleo (66)
Vivstavarvsvägen 245
12264 Enskede
Sweden
fon +46 (0)8 91 68 92
acarleo@hotmail.com

Lara Chamoun (140)
c/o Rosette Chamoun
Beirut Sorting Center
Beirut International Airport
Beirut 6000
Lebanon

So-Hyon Choe (68, 103)
Dudenstr. 34
D-10965 Berlin
fon +49 (0)30 7 86 77 63

Marta Daul (60)
Böhmestr. 32
D-28215 Bremen
fon +49 (0)421 37 49 05
mdaul@uni-bremen.de

Kerstin Deindörfer (42)
Waldheimstr. 11
D-91126 Schwabach
fon +49 (0)9122 7 72 58
k.deindoerfer@theim.de

Anja Denz (59)
Schlegelstr. 9
D-10115 Berlin
fon +49 (0)30 2 85 93 01
denzanja@hotmail.com

Isil Döneray (127)
Bolahenk Sok. Eralko Apt. no. 2 D.5
Findikli Istanbul
Turkey
fon +90 (0)212 2 51 94 70

Sandra Dörfler (48, 77)
Schillerstr. 37
D-76135 Karlsruhe
fon +49 (0)721 84 83 49
doerfler@hfg-karlsruhe.de

Gesine Dorschner (126)
Ganghoferstr. 1
D-82229 Seefeld
fon +49 (0)8152 7 84 43
ute.dorschner@5sl.org

Natasa Drakula (22)
Sophienstr. 6
D-10178 Berlin
fon +49 (0)30 28 59 88 83
drakula@snafu.de

Tess Dryza (135)
176 Beattie Street
Balmain, NSW 2041
Australia
fon +61 (0)2 97 15 82 37
ripe@one.net.au

Bele Ducke (105)
Am Iderfenngraben 3
D-13156 Berlin
fon +49 (0)30 4 77 26 76
dbele@hotmail.com

Christian Dworak (34)
Düppelstr. 54
D-24105 Kiel
fon +49 (0)431 8 11 36
dworak@kiel.jessenlenz.com

Andrew Ecclestone (34)

Silke Eggers (133)
Papenkamp 24
D-24114 Kiel
fon +49 (0)431 6 61 41 30
silke@muthesius.de

Sheila Elkins (111)
130 Avon Road
Haverford, PA 19041
USA
fon +1 610 6 49 89 22

Martin Ernsting (150)
Borcherdingstr. 1
D-28757 Bremen
fon +49 (0)173 2 01 73 70
martin@dust.de

Maike Freiberg (36)
Schifferstr. 33a
D-60596 Frankfurt/Main
fon +49 (0)69 96 20 03 64

Marta Josa Fresno (96)
Freser 11 1-2
08026 Barcelona, Spain
fon +34 (0)93 4 55 91 57

Irina Futivic (86)
Rua do Carmo 31-6A
1200-093 Lisboa
Portugal
fon +351 (0)1 3 46 09 42
ifutivic@mailcity.com

Damir Gamulin (12)
IV Maksimirsko naselje 32
10 000 Zagreb
Croatia
fon +385 (0)1 22 27 23
gamba13@yahoo.com

Dennis Gleason (106)
1011 W. 23rd #103
Austin, TX 78705
USA
dennisg@mail.utexas.edu

Christiane Gödde (95)
Landswehrstr. 15
D-44147 Dortmund
fon +49 (0)231 82 53 26

Katja Gretzinger (84)
Austr. 22
CH-8045 Zürich
Switzerland
fon +41 (0)1 4 51 88 60
katja.gretzinger@smile.ch

Constanze Greve (77, 89, 101)
c/o Graf
Klauprechtstr. 20
D-76137 Karlsruhe
fon +49 (0)721 9 82 26 17
cgreve@gmx.de

Tobias Kazumichi Grime (37)
PO Box A2384
New South Wales 2000
Australia
fon +61 (0)2 94 89 86 78
toby@ebom.org
www.kazumichi.com

Yvonne Günther (144)
Friedrichstr. 27
D-40217 Düsseldorf
fon +49 (0)211 38 44 75 11

Marc Guddorp (94)
Taubenstr. 3
D-48415 Münster
fon +49 (0)251 66 59 87
guddorp@aol.com

Micah Hahn (115)
1623 Raymond Ave.
Hermosa Beach, CA 90254
USA
fon +1 310 3 72 69 32
micah@dvsshoecompany.com

Gerd Häußler (67)
Ortsstr. 62
D-89081 Ulm
fon +49 (0)7304 79 04
haeussler-g@hfg-gmuend.de

Indra Häußler (36)
Pallaswiesenstr. 57 Zi. 206
D-64293 Darmstadt
fon +49 (0)6151 29 41 42
indra.h@excite.com

Jan Haux (18, 49)
Kriegsstr. 274
D-76135 Karlsruhe
fon +49 (0)721 85 45 00
jhaux@hfg-karlsruhe.de

Judith Hehl (117)
Schillerstr. 27
D-76135 Karlsruhe
fon +49 (0)721 9 20 49 57

Katharina v. Hellberg (21)
Heinrich-Vogl-Str. 14
D-81479 München
fon +49 (0)89 79 77 99

Jörg Hemker (46)
Neptunstr. 2
D-44388 Dortmund
fon +49 (0)231 69 40 29

Carsten Hermann (117)
Schillerstr. 27
D-76135 Karlsruhe
fon +49 (0)721 9 20 49 57

Andreas Hidber (19)
Mattstück Weg 8
CH-4153 Reinach
Switzerland
fon +41 (0)61 7 11 51 53
ahidber@datacom.ch

Eduardo Cortada Hindersein (130)
Aribau, 254 1-2
08006 Barcelona
Spain
fon +34 (0)93 2 00 89 97

Bambang Irawan (134)
Jalan Muara Karang Blck E3S no. 12
Jakarta Utara 14450
Indonesia
fon +62 (0)21 6 62 20 63

Elena Isaeva (50)
Vorovsky Street 83-6
610017 Kirov
Russia
fon +7 095 4 06 66 27

Ellen Jacoby (88)
Kohlhökerstr. 12
D-28203 Bremen
fon +49 (0)421 3 37 87 45
designkantine@hotmail.com

Miriam Kaddoura (28)
American University of Beirut
PO BOX 11-0236/1138
Beirut
Lebanon
fon +961 (0)3 31 17 71
mirakaddoura@hotmail.com

Annika Kaltenthaler (129)
Kirchweg 31
D-90419 Nürnberg
fon +49 (0)171 4 47 75 17
annika.kaltenthaler@ideenhaus.de

Sonja Kampczyk (78)
Grünewalderberg 27
D-42105 Wuppertal
fon +49 (0)202 30 69 37
sonja@fkk-design.com

Svetlana Katargina (64)
Koshtoagynza Street 2-15
117454 Moskow
Russia
fon +7 095 1 21 38 86

Silke Kemnitz (42)
Friedenstr. 4
D-90765 Fürth
fon +49 (0)911 9 79 91 78
silke.kemnitz@da-kapo.de

Christoph Kerschner (116)
J.W. Kleinstr. 72/5/28
A-4040 Linz
Austria
fon +43 (0)732 2 55 02 28
christoph.kerschner@commit.at

Elmar Keweloh (150)
Böhmestr. 11
D-28215 Bremen
fon +49 (0)421 3 76 09 18
soulcagedp@cs.com

Tobias Klauser (102)
Forchstr. 127
CH-8032 Zürich
Switzerland
fon +41 (0)1 3 81 87 29

Ingrid Klinger (60)
Am Dobben 52
D-28203 Bremen
fon +49 (0)421 7 94 98 87
iklinger@uni-bremen.de

Sabine Kobel (29)
Sommerhalde 9
D-78662 Bösingen
fon +49 (0)7404 74 05

Laurent Lacour (124)
Wittelsbacherallee 76
D-60385 Frankfurt/Main
fon +49 (0)69 44 29 75
laurent@stud.uni-frankfurt.de

Friederike Lambers (47)
Ostendorpstr. 26
D-28203 Bremen
fon +49 (0)421 7 94 83 72
jungundpfeffer@t-online.de

Chae Lee (90)

Sebastian Lemm (68)
c/o Atelier 41
Bundesallee 89
D-12161 Berlin
fon +49 (0)30 8 51 61 78
atelier41@aol.com

Kiyo Matsumoto (27)
209 E. 25th St. # 2F
Minneapolis, MN 55404
USA

Michael Meyer (150)
Upper Borg 155
D-28357 Bremen
fon +49 (0)421 27 59 46
soulcagedp@cs.com

Dorthe Meinhardt (47)
Ostertorsteinweg 67
D-28203 Bremen
fon +49 (0)421 7 94 05 35
dorthe@propellers.org

Esther Mildenberger (104)
138 Southgate Road
London N1 3HX
Great Britain
fon +44 (0)171 9 23 15 46
emildenberger@hotmail.com

Maryam Miremadi (36)
Bahnhofstr. 42
D-35390 Giessen
fon +49 (0)641 9 71 57 66
maryam_miremadi@jvm-main.de

Jacek Mrowczyk (100)
ul. Widok 22 m.6
31-564 Kraków, Poland

Nina Murray (68)
Wilhelm-Bonn-Str. 18
D-61476 Kronberg
fon +49 (0)6173 92 94 97

Bürkan Özkan (114)

Alexandra Ostrovskaja (65)
Dmitrovskoje Chaussee 43-1-291
127550 Moskow, Russia
fon +7 095 9 76 98 04

Dominik Pietsch (126)
Meringer-Zellerstr. 28
D-86415 Meringen
fon +49 (0)173 2 31 62 04
pietsch-d@hfg-gmuend.de

Chris Pollak (67)
Platanenweg 43
D-73312 Geislingen
fon +49 (0)170 5 24 74 42
pollak-c@hfg-gmuend.de

Michael Pollard (120)

Sibylle Reichelt (14)
5-Büro für Gestaltung
Friedrich-Ebert-Str. 82
D-34119 Kassel
fon +49 (0)561 73 96 20

Sandra Reichert (126)
Riemannstr. 1
D-73447 Oberkochen
fon +49 (0)7171 8 87 15
sandra-reichert@hfg-gmuend.de

Mirja Rosenau
Im Wiesengrund 11
D-28790 Schwanewede
fon +49 (0)421 62 15 11
mrosenau@hfg-karlsruhe.de

Agnes Rozanska-Haager (40)
Dobbenweg 5
D-28203 Bremen
fon +49 (0)421 7 94 01 35
haager.rozanska@t-online.de

Iris Rütten (108)
Horngasse 12
D-52064 Aachen
fon +49 (0)241 3 84 14
iris.ruetten@dialup.fh-aachen.de

Eun Ryu (98)
260-88 Songbuk 2-Dong, Dongbuk-qu,
Seoul 136-022, Korea
fon +82 (0)2 7 43 80 65
speed74@ag.co.kr

Stefanie Saxe (145)
Meppener Str. 5
D-45145 Essen
fon +49 (0)201 32 10 69
stefanie.saxe@uni-essen.de

Irma Schick (70)
Marcobrunnenstr. 16
D-65197 Wiesbaden
fon +49 (0)611 30 97 69

Katrin Schlüsener (112)
Alexanderstr. 170
D-70180 Stuttgart
fon +49 (0)711 60 40 20
k.schluesener@abk-stuttgart.de

Annette Schmidt (109)
Hebelstr. 13
D-78315 Radolfzell
fon +49 (0)7732 91 05 71
a_schmidti@yahoo.com

Antje Schnier (132)
Muhliusstr. 83
D-24103 Kiel
fon +49 (0)431 55 48 81
aschnier@muthesius.de

Anke Schröder (108)
Münstereifeler Str. 25
D-50937 Köln
fon +49 (0)221 4 20 13 80
anke.s@netcologne.de

Esmeralda Schürch (30)
Weststr. 20
Ch-8003 Zürich
Switzerland
fon +41 (0)1 4 51 85 30

Ellen Schweizer (136)
Danzigerstr. 191
D-10407 Berlin
fon +49 (0)30 42 85 85 24

Ta-Li Shieh (76)
#3, Lane 62, Ta-Chi St.
Taipei
Taiwan ROC
fon +886 (0)2 25 33 81 51

Kelly Stevens (20, 26)
3906A Willbert Road
Austin, Texas 78751
USA
fon +1 512 3 74 15 77
kelly@scaredypants.com

Dorothee Stickling (52)
Eigelstein 73
D-50668 Köln
fon +49 (0)172 6 63 04 69
djstick73@hotmail.com

Walter Stromberger (116)
Harrachstr. 34/3
A-4020 Linz
Austria
fon +43 (0)732 79 75 15
walter.stromberger@commit.at

Petra Sutter (129)
Bismarckstr. 81
D-70197 Stuttgart
fon +49 (0)711 6 36 84 07
sutter@sanshine.de

Erkut Terliksiz (44)

Carola Thölke (75)
Müggenkampstr. 35a
D-20257 Hamburg
fon +49 (0)40 43 27 26 94

Andrea Tinnes (32)
Perlerstr. 9
D-66663 Merzig-Weiler
fon +49 (0)6869 4 60
andreatinnes@hotmail.com

Mindi Tirabassi (122)
34 Sidney Place, Garden Apt.
Brooklyn, NY 11201
USA
fon/fax +1 718 8 52 66 42
mtirabassi@mindspring.com

Jochen Tratz (128)
Friedrich-Spee-Str. 27
D-97072 Würzburg
fon +49 (0)931 88 40 53
g026@mail.fh-wuerzburg.de

Maike Truschkowsi (14)
5-Büro für Gestaltung
Friedrich-Ebert-Str. 82
D-34119 Kassel
fon +49 (0)561 73 96 20

Amy Unikewicz (87)
131 Washington Street #202
Norwalk, CT 06854
USA
fon +1 203 8 31 08 04
aunikewicz@student.schoolofvisualarts.edu

Kathrin Wackersreuther (72)
Dachauerstr. 263
D-80637 München
fon +49 (0)89 15 98 21 33
kathrin.wackersreuther@munich.netsurf.de

Monika Waigand (132)
Plöner Landstr. 7
D-24238 Mucheln
fon +49 (0)4384 59 93 10
waigandm@muthesius.de

Stefanie Weigele (92)
Hollerstr. 20/22
D-28203 Bremen
fon +49 (0)421 7 94 11 32

Bianca Wessalowski (45)
Ostendorpstr. 9
D-28203 Bremen
fon +49 (0)421 70 23 61
biancaw@uni-bremen.de

Christopher Wiehl (144)
Friedrichstr. 27
D-40217 Düsseldorf
fon +49 (0)211 38 44 75 11
chezwiehl@rocketmail.com

Ulrich Wimmer (61)
Kaiserstr. 208
D-44143 Dortmund
fon +49 (0)231 59 00 77

Nikolai Wolff (138)
Richard-Wagner-Str. 11-13
D-28209 Bremen
fon +49 (0)421 7 23 28

Poppy Yaneswari (110)
Puri Kartika AE 16
Ciledug Tangerang 15152
Indonesia
fon +62 (0)21 7 32 08 42

Stanley Yip (37)
Unit 3A/150 Dean St.
Strathfield South, NSW 2136
Australia
fon +61 (0)2 97 42 66 86
info@yippyio.com.au
www.yippyio.com.au

Taline Yozgatian (123)
Horizon Bldg. Achrafieh
Geitawi Beirut
Lebanon
fon +961 (0)1 44 57 46

Andreas Zeischegg (67)
Oblatterwallstr. 22h
D-86153 Augsburg
fon +49 (0)821 51 91 07
zeischegg-a@hfg-gmuend.de

Trudi Zwick (72)
Gaisenbergstr. 33
D-89073 Ulm
fon +49 (0)731 9 21 74 68
trudizwick@hotmail.com

Prof. Dieter und Ingeborg Rams-Stiftung Kronberg

Thank You: Ingeborg and Dieter Rams

 Thanks to the people who rescued this book:
Helge Aszmoneit, Lutz Dietzhold, Stefan Elsner, Tanja Gaul,
Anja Holle, Eckhard Jung, Dorthe Meinhardt, Kay Michalak, Boris Müller,
Jens Neuber, Peter Rea, Till Teenck

Special thanks to:
Friederike Lambers and Ella Lorenz

	output[02]:	International Yearbook for awarded works of Graphic Design Students
		Internationales Jahrbuch für prämierte Arbeiten von Grafik-Design Student/innen
	Editors:	
	Herausgeber:	Florian Pfeffer
		+
		Dieter Kretschmann
		for German Design Council
		für den Rat für Formgebung
	Contributing Editors:	Sheila de Bretteville
		Irma Boom
		Richard Doust
		Neil Grant
		Steven Heller
		Ken Hiebert
		Werner Jeker
		Eckhard Jung
		William Longhauser
		Leila Musfy
		Hanny Kardinata
		John Kortbawi
		Peter Rea
		Louise Sandhaus
		Ahn Sang-Soo
		Robyn Stacey
		Chris Treweek
		Teal Triggs
	Design:	jung und pfeffer
		visual communication, Bremen
	Translation:	
	Übersetzung:	SATS
		Translation Services, Ehingen
		Katja Steiner, Bruce Almberg
	Publishing and Distribution:	
	Verlag und Vertrieb:	Verlag Hermann Schmidt Mainz
		Robert-Koch-Straße 8
		55129 Mainz
		Germany
		in cooperation with
		PAGE
		Zeitschrift für digitale Mediengestaltung
		magazine for digital media production
	©	Florian Pfeffer, Bremen
	ISBN	3-87439-487-5
		Printed in Germany

All rights reserved. No part of this publication may be reproduced or transmitted in any form ar by any means electronical or mechanical, including photography or any information storage and retrieval system. Das Werk einschließlich aller seiner Teile ist urheberrechtlich geschützt. Jede Verwertung außerhalb der engen Grenzen des Urheberrechts ist ohne Zustimmung des Herausgebers unzulässig und strafbar. Das gilt insbesondere für Vervielfältigungen, Übersetzungen und Verarbeitung in elektronischen Systemen.

1→

2→

3→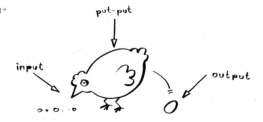

With best regards from the Cartoon Group at the College of Arts Bremen, Germany:
Mit besten Grüßen von der Cartoongruppe der Hochschule für Künste Bremen:
1 Michael Meyer
2 Elmar Keweloh
3 Martin Ernsting

Prof. Bernd Bexte